33 VARIATIONS

BY MOISÉS KAUFMAN

DRAMATISTS
PLAY SERVICE
INC.

SPECIAL NOTE

Anyone receiving permission to produce 33 VARIATIONS is required to give credit to the Author as sole and exclusive Author of the Play on the title page of all programs distributed in connection with performances of the Play and in all instances in which the title of the Play appears for purposes of advertising, publicizing or otherwise exploiting the Play and/or a production thereof. The name of the Author must appear on a separate line, in which no other name appears, immediately beneath the title and in size of type equal to 50% of the size of the largest, most prominent letter used for the title of the Play. No person, firm or entity may receive credit larger or more prominent than that accorded the Author. The following acknowledgment must appear on the title page in all programs distributed in connection with performances of the Play:

Originally produced on Broadway, 2009
by
David Binder
Ruth Hendel   Barbara Whitman
Goldberg/Mills   Latitude Link   Arielle Tepper Madover   Bill Resnick
Eric Schnall   Jayne Baron Sherman   Willis/True Love Productions
and
Tectonic Theater Project
(Greg Reiner, Executive Director; Dominick Balletta, General Manager; Jeffrey LaHoste, Senior Producer)

SPECIAL NOTE ON MUSIC

A PDF of the piano score as edited by Diane Walsh is required for production and is available through the Play Service for $10.00. There is no additional fee for the use of this music.

SPECIAL NOTE ON IMAGES

A DVD containing images for projection is optional for production and is available through the Play Service for $35.00, plus shipping and handling. The nonprofessional fee for the use of these images is $25.00 per performance.

Several images required for production are protected under copyright by the Beethoven-Haus Bonn, so the Play Service is unable to distribute them. For rights to use those images, contact the Beethoven-Haus Bonn directly.

This play is dedicated to my beloved parents
Dora Akerman and José Kaufman.

ACKNOWLEDGMENTS

Many people and organizations worked on 33 VARIATIONS during its birthing process. And many more talked to me about it, guided me through the musicological aspects of the piece and acted in the workshops where I wrote it. To all of them my most heartfelt thanks. Here are but a few:

First and foremost, to Dr. William Kinderman, the world's greatest expert on the *Diabelli Variations*. His patience with a neophyte, his kindness and intelligence made this play possible. To Dr. Katherine Syer, a musicologist of great intelligence and erudition who was always ready to supply further insight into Beethoven's work.

To the Sundance Theatre Lab (Philip Himberg, Robert Redford, and Ken Brecher) where the first act of the piece was born.

To Ari Edelson and the Orchard Project, who gave us time to develop the play.

To Molly Smith, who was the first to believe in the piece and who nurtured it at Arena Stage until it was ready to be seen.

To Mark Bly, dramaturg extraordinaire. He was kind, patient, and brilliant; I am in his debt.

To Eric Rosen for his dramturgical advice in the early stages of this play. It was invaluable.

To Kelli Simpkins, who was instrumental in defining the role of Clara. Her masterful and inspiring dramaturgy on the play made it better.

To Christopher Ashley, for our lovely time at La Jolla. His keen eye and kind manner left their mark on our journey.

To David Binder, producer savant. Thank you! I adore you.

To my teacher and longtime mentor, Stephen Wangh, whose insight and advice came, as always, at the most opportune time.

To the actors who participated in the workshops: Mercedes Herrero, Kelly Simpkins, Grant James Vargas, David Chandler, Emily Donahoe, David Patrick Kelly, Scott Barrow, Mary Beth Peil, Helen Carey, Jayne Atkinson, Laura Odeh, and Greg Keller.

To the virtuosic Diane Walsh, who taught me about playing the variations and about living in them.

And last but most importantly, to everyone at Tectonic Theater Project who made this play possible to begin with. Especially Dominick Balletta, Greg Reiner, Jimmy Maize, Tiffany Redmon, Luke Harlan, and Jeffrey LaHoste. As well as our board: Kevin Jennings, Tim Wu, Jeffrey LaHoste, Amy Stursberg, Ralph Bryan, Philip Gallo, Michael Graziano, Violy McCausland-Seve, David Melançon, Cathy Renna, and Ted Trimpa.

All of their work is in the body of the play. Thank you.

AUTHOR'S NOTE

Although this play is based on a historical event, namely the birth of the *Diabelli Variations*, I have chosen to explore this story from a fictional perspective. Thus, this play is not a reconstruction of a historical event; rather, it's a series of variations on a moment in a life.

One other thought. In addition to the characters listed in the script, there are two more characters in the play: one, the music of Beethoven's *Diabelli Variations* which plays over the course of the story—whenever possible, it should be played live; and two, the images of the original Beethoven sketches projected throughout the piece—they tell their own story.

33 VARIATIONS was developed by Tectonic Theater Project with assistance from the Sundance Institute Theatre Program, the Orchard Project theatre residency program, the Georgetown University Theater and Performance Studies program, and the Krannert Center for the Performing Arts at the University of Illinois, Urbana-Champaign.

33 VARIATIONS premiered on August 30, 2007, at Arena Stage, Washington, DC (Molly Smith, Artistic Director; Guy Bergquist, Interim Managing Director; Alan Filderman, Casting Director). It was directed by Moisés Kaufman; the dramaturg was Mark Bly; the set design was by Derek McLane; the costume design was by Janice Pytel; the lighting design was by David Lander; the sound design was by André J. Pluess; the projection design was by Jeff Sugg; the hair and wig design was by Charles LaPointe; the choreographer was Peter Anastos; the stage manager was Meghan Gauger; and production manager was Carey Lawless. The cast was as follows:

DR. KATHERINE BRANDT .... Mary Beth Peil
CLARA BRANDT .... Laura Odeh
MIKE CLARK .... Greg Keller
LUDWIG VAN BEETHOVEN .... Graeme Malcolm
ANTON DIABELLI .... Don Amendolia
DR. GERTRUDE LADENBURGER .... Susan Kellermann
ANTON SCHINDLER .... Erik Steele
PIANIST .... Diane Walsh

33 VARIATIONS was produced in 2008 by the La Jolla Playhouse in La Jolla, California (Christopher Ashley, Artistic Director; Joan Cumming, Interim Managing Director). It was directed by Moisés Kaufman; the dramaturg was Mark Bly; the set design was by Derek McLane; the costume design was by Janice Pytel; the lighting design was by David Lander; the sound design was by André J. Pluess; the projection design was by Jeff Sugg; the hair and wig design was by Charles LaPointe; the choreographer was Daniel Pelzig; the production stage manager was Linda Marvel; and the assistant stage manager was Melissa Spengler. The cast was as follows:

DR. KATHERINE BRANDT .... Jayne Atkinson
CLARA BRANDT .... Laura Odeh
MIKE CLARK .... Ryan King
LUDWIG VAN BEETHOVEN .... Zach Grenier
ANTON DIABELLI .... Don Amendolia
DR. GERTRUDE LADENBURGER .... Susan Kellermann
ANTON SCHINDLER .... Erik Steele
PIANIST .... Diane Walsh

33 VARIATIONS received its New York premiere on Broadway at the Eugene O'Neill Theatre on March 9, 2009. It was directed by Moisés Kaufman; the dramaturg was Mark Bly; the set design was by Derek McLane; the costume design was by Janice Pytel; the lighting design was by David Lander; the sound design was by André J. Pluess; the projection design was by Jeff Sugg; the hair and wig design was by Charles LaPointe; the choreographer was Daniel Pelzig; the assistant director was Jimmy Maize; the production stage manager was Linda Marvel; the stage manager was Pat Sosnow; and additional costumes were by David C. Woolard. The cast was as follows:

DR. KATHERINE BRANDT .... Jane Fonda
CLARA BRANDT .... Samantha Mathis
MIKE CLARK .... Colin Hanks
LUDWIG VAN BEETHOVEN .... Zach Grenier
ANTON DIABELLI .... Don Amendolia
DR. GERTRUDE LADENBURGER .... Susan Kellermann
ANTON SCHINDLER .... Erik Steele
PIANIST/MUSICAL DIRECTOR .... Diane Walsh
ENSEMBLE .... Scott Barrow, Emily Donahoe, Caitlin O'Connell, Michael Winther

CHARACTERS

DR. KATHERINE BRANDT, a musicologist

CLARA BRANDT, her daughter

MIKE CLARK, a nurse

LUDWIG VAN BEETHOVEN, a composer

ANTON DIABELLI, a music publisher

DR. GERTRUDE LADENBURGER, a librarian

ANTON SCHINDLER, Beethoven's secretary

TIME

1819, 1823, and the present.

PLACE

New York, U.S.A.; Bonn, Germany; and Vienna, Austria.

33 VARIATIONS

ACT ONE

Variation: "Theme"

A shaft of light comes up on a beautiful black grand piano. A pianist enters. She crosses to the piano, sits and begins to play the "Theme" by Anton Diabelli. A projection appears with the word "Theme."

Before the first half of the theme repeats, Katherine Brandt enters holding her purse. She looks around, sizing up the room. She is in what appears to be a waiting room. Clara Brandt enters and stands beside her. The waltz ends. Katherine addresses the audience—an aside that Clara doesn't hear.

KATHERINE. Let us begin with the primary cause of things.
Let us begin with how something came about.
Why it came about in that particular way
and became what it is.

Pause.

For me, it begins in Vienna, in 1819.

CLARA. Mom.

KATHERINE. *(Still in her own world talking to the audience.)* For me, it begins with a music publisher by the name of Anton Diabelli.

CLARA. MOM!

KATHERINE. This music publisher has written a small waltz that will…change everything!

CLARA. MOM?

KATHERINE. *(Brought back to the present.)* What is it?

CLARA. Have you heard a word I've said?

KATHERINE. Yes.

CLARA. What did I say?

KATHERINE. You said that…that…they'll call us in soon.

CLARA. No. I said that everyone else who was here before us has gone in. So we're next.

KATHERINE. We've been here for two hours.

CLARA. I know. We're next.

Pause.

Do you need anything?

KATHERINE. No. Thank you. I'm fine.
I have to be at the office by three.

CLARA. You'll make it.

KATHERINE. Don't you have to be at work?

CLARA. I told them I'd be late.

KATHERINE. You can leave, Clara. I've done this many times before.

Katherine struggles with buttoning her jacket.

CLARA. Here, let me help you.

Clara tries to help Katherine with the buttons. But Katherine doesn't let her.

KATHERINE. Thank you. I can do it.

She succeeds. The nurse, Mike, enters.

MIKE. Hello there. So sorry about the delay.

KATHERINE. It's been two hours.

MIKE. Yes, I'm very sorry. It's been a madhouse here today.

KATHERINE. And who are you?

MIKE. Mike.

KATHERINE. Where's Gary?

MIKE. It's his day off. You got me today.

KATHERINE. Are you a doctor?

MIKE. No. I'm a nurse.

Katherine shoots Clara a glance.

CLARA. But, you'll just be administering the tests, right?

MIKE. Yeah, I'll only do the tests.

CLARA. *(To Katherine.)* He'll only do the tests. *(To Mike.)* OK.

MIKE. *(To Clara.)* So, you must be Katherine Brandt.

KATHERINE. I am Dr. Brandt.

MIKE. Oh. OK. Come this way, please.

Clara tries to follow them.

Excuse me. You have to wait out here.

CLARA. Well, I would like to come in with her.

MIKE. No, we're going to examine her. So, you better stay here.

CLARA. Just so you know, because my mother is not going to tell you, she wants to travel in a week.

KATHERINE. Why wouldn't I tell him? I'd tell him.

I'm supposed to travel in a week.

CLARA. To Bonn

MIKE. Where is that?

CLARA. In Germany.

KATHERINE. Which is in Europe.

MIKE. Thank you.

I don't see any problem with it right now. You look fine to me. But let's see what these show.

When was your last visit?

KATHERINE. Four months ago.

CLARA. Apparently she was told she had to come every two months.

MIKE. She looks fine to me.

CLARA. I really think she should postpone her trip to Bonn a bit. Don't you think?

MIKE. I'm a nurse, not a travel agent.

Katherine laughs.

CLARA. Can I talk to you for a minute in private?

MIKE. I don't think so. Your mother is my patient. Not you.

KATHERINE. Go ahead. Otherwise we'll be here all day.

Mike and Clara exit. Katherine addresses the audience again.

I begin my search in Vienna, in 1819.

The effects of the French Revolution are still being felt all over Europe and the ideas of freedom and equality are galvanizing people's minds.

The world is poised to enter the modern era.

In that year, Byron, Goethe, Victor Hugo, Keats, and Shelley have all written new books.

In Vienna, music is everywhere.

Schubert, Beethoven, Liszt, and Czerny are all composing new works.

Amidst all this, one event captures my imagination more than all the others.

A music publisher by the name of Anton Diabelli extends an invitation.

Diabelli enters to a short introduction played by the pianist. His garments are too fashionable and his hair has too much balm.

DIABELLI. An invitation!

To the fifty GREATEST composers in Vienna.

My dear Musicians,

I am enclosing in this letter a new waltz of my own making.

The waltz begins to play. He listens with great pleasure to his own composition. The music continues under the dialogue.

KATHERINE. He was a great music publisher, but not so great a composer.

DIABELLI. I composed it but a few days ago.

And I wish to invite each of you to compose one variation on my theme.

Once I receive your variations, I will publish them all in one handsome volume that I promise will be a beautiful and popular book.

KATHERINE. He knew it would sell well. After all, for the price of one book, the music lover would receive fifty compositions by the best composers in Vienna.

DIABELLI. I hope you will find in my waltz a worthy and inspiring theme.

KATHERINE. All of whom would have immortalized Diabelli's tiny waltz.

DIABELLI. And of course, I will compensate each of you for the variation that you contribute.

I eagerly await your reply.

Yours sincerely, Anton Diabelli

Music Publisher

Of the firm Diabelli, Cappi and Company.

KATHERINE. All the composers accepted Diabelli's invitation and went to work on a variation of his less-than-stellar waltz.

All the composers except one.

Schindler enters. A short introduction played by the pianist.

SCHINDLER. Signor Diabelli —

KATHERINE. Beethoven's reply comes via his secretary, Anton Schindler.

SCHINDLER. The master has received your charming and melodic waltz, along with your request for him to write one variation on it.

KATHERINE. Beethoven took one look at it and hated it.

SCHINDLER. Although this project is a very intriguing proposition, and the master is very curious about it…

KATHERINE. He called it a "*Schusterfleck.*" A cobbler's patch.

He found it commonplace.

SCHINDLER. At this time, he is inundated with other commissions,

KATHERINE. He vehemently refused to have anything to do with it.

SCHINDLER. So he must regretfully decline your very kind invitation.

KATHERINE. Thank you very much.

SCHINDLER. Sincerely,

KATHERINE. Yours truly,

SCHINDLER. Your servant,

KATHERINE. Etc., etc.

SCHINDLER. Anton Schindler.

SCHINDLER and KATHERINE. Friend of Beethoven.

KATHERINE. *(Continuing.)* That's actually what his calling card said.

DIABELLI. Herr Schindler, I am asking but for one variation—just to have his name on it.

SCHINDLER. I am sorry, his mind is completely occupied with other commissions.

KATHERINE. But then something happened to Beethoven.

The sound of Beethoven whispering comes from offstage. Schindler looks offstage trying to discern what Beethoven is saying.

SCHINDLER. What?

Beethoven whispers again.

What?

Beethoven whispers again.

What do you mean?

KATHERINE. *(Over Beethoven's whispering.)* ...History doesn't record what he said.

Beethoven whispers again.

SCHINDLER. But I already told him?
Are you certain?

Whispers again.

Fine.

Whispers again.

Fine!

Back to Diabelli.

Dear Signor Diabelli,

The master has asked me to come see you in person. I will be in your offices tomorrow at three o'clock.

DIABELLI. For what purpose?

SCHINDLER. Until then I remain most sincerely yours,
Anton Schindler,
Friend of Beethoven.

DIABELLI. Thank you, yes. I will see you then.

Schindler and Diabelli exit.

KATHERINE. Beethoven changed his mind and became obsessed with this waltz: He devoted the next three years of his life to it.

He did not write one variation. Instead, he wrote thirty-three variations on Diabelli's theme! His longest piece for solo piano and what many musicians consider the most important work in variation form.

Pause.

This obsession of Beethoven's baffles me.

What was it about this mediocre waltz that so captured his imagination?

At this point in his life, Beethoven is only tackling major works. He has very little time left. And yet he chooses this insignificant waltz as his next project. Why?

I will be leaving in a few days to go to Bonn.

There at the Beethoven archive, I will be able to look at his diaries and his sketches.

I have to understand why a genius became obsessed with mediocrity.

Mike and Clara return.

MIKE. I'm ready for you, Dr. Brandt.

KATHERINE. Who won?

CLARA. He did. I'll wait here.

KATHERINE. Are you sure we can't call Gary?

MIKE. Yes. But if it makes you feel any better, you can call me Gary.

KATHERINE. Great! A funny nurse!

Katherine and Mike exit. Lights fade as the pianist plays Variation #1. Projection: "Variation #1." During the music we journey to Beethoven's house.

Variation: "Eavesdropping"

As the music plays, a door is ajar. Loud and tempestuous music pours into the stage from a room offstage right.

Beethoven is inside that room, unseen by us, composing Variation #1. Strange sounds are coming out of the room in addition to the piano. As he composes, he is shouting the tunes out of key, or humming loudly. Schindler enters from the opposite side of the stage, slowly walks towards the doorway, eavesdropping. He's mesmerized and intrigued by the music. He approaches the door, very worried that he will be caught eavesdropping on the master.

Suddenly, the sound of a metal tray falling on the floor. Music stops abruptly.

BEETHOVEN. *(Offstage.) Scheiße.*

The music stops abruptly right before the end of Variation #1. Schindler tries to retreat so as not to be discovered. Offstage:

Schindler!

SCHINDLER. Yes, master!

A tray of food is handed through the open doorway. Beethoven is still not seen. Schindler takes the tray and starts off.

Thank you, master.

BEETHOVEN. *(Offstage.)* And Schindler!

SCHINDLER. *(Returning obediently.)* Yes, master.

BEETHOVEN. *(Offstage.)* I need more paper.

SCHINDLER. Master, Herr Offenheimer says he won't give us any more paper.

We owe him too much money.

BEETHOVEN. Then get it from Schtuphaffar.

SCHINDLER. He won't give us any more paper because we owe him too much money.

BEETHOVEN. Then get it from Schmitz!

SCHINDLER. You called him a sniveling pig donkey.

BEETHOVEN. And I need more ink!

SCHINDLER. Yes, master!

BEETHOVEN. And Schindler.

Schindler returns again.

Open the shutters! It's too dark in here.

SCHINDLER. Yes, master.

Schindler hurries away. The pianist plays Variation #2. Projection: "Variation #2." As the music plays, the stage becomes Katherine's bedroom.

Variation: "Research"

Clara is waiting in Katherine's bedroom. There is a half-packed suitcase on a table. Katherine enters holding her laptop with her one good hand.

KATHERINE. Here it is. It crashed. I can't get it to work. I need you to take it to the place in midtown and make sure they have it ready by tomorrow.

CLARA. Sure, no problem.

Katherine continues packing her clothes into her suitcase.

Do you have your meds?

KATHERINE. I do.

Pause.

CLARA. Do you have the numbers for the doctors in Bonn?

KATHERINE. Yes.

CLARA. Good.

Pause.

Do you need help with that?

KATHERINE. No, I'm good, thank you. I'm almost done.
    Did you cut your hair?

CLARA. No.

KATHERINE. It looks...different.

CLARA. No. It's the same.

KATHERINE. You have such beautiful hair.

Pause.

I wish you did something with it.

CLARA. Do you need anything else?

KATHERINE. No. Thank you.

Pause. Katherine packs.

CLARA. I'm going to ask you this one more time. Are you sure you should go now? Why don't you wait six months and see how you feel?

KATHERINE. Who knows what state I'll be in in six months.
    Besides, I've had to call in favors from every music scholar I know to get access to the archive.

CLARA. But you heard what the nurse said.

KATHERINE. He said it would be better if I wasn't alone. Which I won't be. There's going to be colleagues there.
    Did it make you feel uncomfortable the way he kept looking at you?

CLARA. Please! That nurse?

KATHERINE. Yes, that nurse. He was staring at you.

CLARA. No, he wasn't.

KATHERINE. In the exam room he kept asking me questions about you.

CLARA. Oh, Mom.

KATHERINE. It took him fifteen minutes to find my vein.

CLARA. Mom, he seemed like he knew what he was doing.

KATHERINE. Clara, he dropped my urine sample.

Clara giggles.

Yes, you should date that guy. He fits the profile of your last three boyfriends.

Pause.

CLARA. Mom, maybe I should come with you.

KATHERINE. What about *Hedda Gabler*?

CLARA. My costumes are done, my assistant can take it from here.
    Besides, I'm looking into a few other things. I'm thinking of apprenticing a set designer.

Silence.

What?

KATHERINE. I thought you liked being a costume designer.

CLARA. I do.

KATHERINE. You can't excel at anything if you keep changing careers.

CLARA. I excel at changing careers.

KATHERINE. I think that's a great idea. That way you'll always be mediocre at everything.

Beat. Clara's about to explode, but chooses to remain on subject.

CLARA. What happens if you get weaker? What happens if you fall?

KATHERINE. I'm not on my deathbed!

CLARA. I never said you were.

KATHERINE. No. But you're acting like it.

CLARA. OK, I'm sorry.

I don't understand why you can't do your research here. When you wrote your book on Mozart, you didn't fly off to Vienna.

KATHERINE. Because Mozart composed in his head.

Beethoven composed on paper. So there are thousands and thousands of sketches that record his every thought, his every compositional idea. And they're in Bonn. It's the only hope I have of understanding why he did it. I *have* to go.

CLARA. Is this really how you want to spend this time?

KATHERINE. How else?

Variation: "Negotiating Genius"

Schindler enters Diabelli's office.

SCHINDLER. Signor Diabelli, the master has decided he doesn't want to write one variation on your waltz.

DIABELLI. Yes. So you said.

SCHINDLER. Now he's considering writing a set of several variations on it.

DIABELLI. What?

SCHINDLER. Yes, Diabelli. Fortune smiles upon you.

Lights up on Diabelli's office; they both cross into it.

DIABELLI. A set of variations!

SCHINDLER. That's what he asked me to tell you.

DIABELLI. What wonderful news. And how many variations did he have in mind?

SCHINDLER. Six or seven.

DIABELLI. That many?

SCHINDLER. Indeed.

DIABELLI. But Schindler, I'm confused. Yesterday he didn't have time to write one variation. Today he wants to write seven. Why did the master change his mind?

SCHINDLER. G_d only knows his reasons. But there you are.

DIABELLI. That's wonderful. We would love to publish seven variations by Beethoven. It may even merit its own book.

SCHINDLER. It certainly will.
Of course an undertaking of this magnitude will take many hours of work.

DIABELLI. Yes.

SCHINDLER. Which the master will be devoting to your waltz.

DIABELLI. Yes, what an honor.

SCHINDLER. And he will do all of this for only eighty ducats.

DIABELLI. *(Dreamily.)* Eighty ducats —
Eighty ducats?!

SCHINDLER. In advance.

DIABELLI. In advance?

SCHINDLER. Yes.

DIABELLI. We can't take that kind of a risk.

SCHINDLER. Risk? You're speaking of Beethoven, what is the risk?

DIABELLI. Well, Beethoven has composed nothing of note in the last five years.

SCHINDLER. How dare you!

DIABELLI. It's not me, people are talking.

SCHINDLER. What are people saying?

DIABELLI. That he's finished. That he has nothing more to offer. That he's too ill.

SCHINDLER. People love to talk about other people's maladies. It makes them feel healthy.

Pause. Diabelli looks at Schindler.

DIABELLI. Is any of it true?

SCHINDLER. It is no secret that Beethoven has been ill.

DIABELLI. People who have seen him say he looks like a madman, a beggar.

SCHINDLER. Tread lightly, Diabelli. Or I'll make sure you never get another Beethoven composition.

DIABELLI. Schindler, we can't give you eighty ducats and then not get the composition. That could ruin us.

SCHINDLER. *(Conciliatory.)* Diabelli, it's six or seven variations. And your waltz, your composition, will give birth to a beautiful set of variations by Beethoven!

DIABELLI. You will have forty ducats now, and forty ducats when the work is finished.

They shake hands.

SCHINDLER. I will tell the master.

DIABELLI. Promise me you will keep me informed of his progress at every step.

SCHINDLER. *(Exiting.)* I promise!

DIABELLI. *(Yelling after him.) Buon giorno,* Signor Schindler.

SCHINDLER. *(Peeking back in.) Guten Tag,* Herr Diabelli.

Schindler exits. Pause.

DIABELLI. *(Triumphant!)* A set of variations on my waltz by Ludwig van Beethoven!

Projection: "Variation #4." The pianist plays Variation #4.

Variation: "Two Worlds"

Clara and Mike stand in line in a computer shop. Clara is holding a laptop. After a moment. Mike is wearing a hoodie and a baseball cap. Very different from his nurse uniform.

LOUDSPEAKER. Number sixteen, please come to the counter. Sixteen!

CLARA. Excuse me, what number do you have?

MIKE. Seventeen. What about you?

CLARA. Thirty-four. Have you been waiting long?

MIKE. Um… What day is this?

CLARA. Oh, no.

MIKE. Oh, yes. You in a hurry?

CLARA. Yeah, I need to get my mother's laptop fixed. She is going away on a trip. Are you waiting to get your computer fixed?

MIKE. Yeah…yeah. My laptop. Apparently you're not supposed to drop them.

CLARA. Oh. I'm sorry.

MIKE. Yeah… No, it's actually kind of a nice change. Usually I just come here and pay a hundred and fifty bucks for them to tell me to press Control-Alt-Delete.

CLARA. Oh…yeah, I'm a Mac girl myself.

MIKE. Ooh, I see. Well, we're from totally different worlds then. It'll never work out between us.

Mike playfully punches Clara's arm. She shoots him a look.

Sorry. Oh my G_d. You don't remember me, do you?

CLARA. Um…

MIKE. I examined your mom at the hospital…?

CLARA. Oh! Yeah… Oh, I'm sorry. That was a rough day.

MIKE. Yeah… How's she doing?

CLARA. She's…the same…

MIKE. How long has she been ill?

CLARA. Eight months. But she just told me two weeks ago. She didn't want to worry me.

And she's still going to take that trip. To Bonn.

MIKE. Is that in Germany?

CLARA. Yes. *(Realizing he's pulling her leg.)* Sorry.

MIKE. Well, she's a courageous woman.

CLARA. She has to finish a monograph.

MIKE. A what-o-graph?

CLARA. It's a book she's writing. She has been invited to present a paper on it at a very important music conference.

MIKE. Good for her. Most people when they are diagnosed, they want to stay home and spend time with their family.

Clara, unable to believe he just said that, doesn't respond. Mike, aware of the gigantic faux pas, self-flagellates:

Oh. Sorry. That's not what I meant. I was trying to say how…

CLARA. Not my mother.

MIKE. Ah!

CLARA. We don't have that kind of relationship. She has to finish her monograph.

MIKE. *Oh!*

Uncomfortable pause.

CLARA. I'm sorry, it's Dr…?

MIKE. Mike. No doctor. I'm a nurse.

CLARA. Right.
Clara.

MIKE. Hi. Are you a scholar too?

CLARA. Me? No. I am a costume designer at the moment. But I'm on my way to becoming a set designer.

Mike nods. Uncomfortable pause. What else to talk about? There's obviously some sexual tension between them.

I am going to be here all day, aren't I?

MIKE. Yes, you are.

CLARA. Kinda makes the wait at the hospital seem not so bad.

MIKE. Ah. Touché.

LOUDSPEAKER. Number seventeen, please come to the counter. Seventeen!

MIKE. That's me. Do you want my number?

CLARA. Your number?

He holds up his ticket.

MIKE. Seventeen.

CLARA. Oh no, no, I can't do that.

MIKE. Please, please. I have more time than your mom.

Beat.

I mean she has to catch a plane. You know what I mean.

CLARA. Thank you. Thank you.

Variation: "Fasten Your Seatbelts"

The sound of an airplane taking off is heard and the flight attendant makes the announcement.

FLIGHT ATTENDANT. *Guten Morgen meine Damen und Herren, und wilkommen auf dem Lufthansa Flug acht-null-fünf nach Bonn.*

Katherine enters, looking for her seat. Schindler enters on his way to Hetzendorf, carrying too many of Beethoven's bags. The two cross paths. Katherine finds her seat and puts her bag down. Schindler exits.

Good morning ladies and gentlemen, and welcome again to Lufthansa flight 805 to Bonn. We have now reached our cruising altitude of thirty-five thousand feet. The captain has turned off your seatbelt signs, indicating it is safe to move about the cabin.

The pianist plays Variation #1.

KATHERINE. *(As the music plays.)* This is Variation #1.

In it, Beethoven instructs the pianist with the words *Alla Marcia Maestoso.*

"To be played in the style of a majestic march."

I am fascinated that Beethoven begins his exploration of Diabelli's waltz with a majestic march.

Perhaps he is instructing us:

When beginning a great voyage, one must set aside trepidation, even if we may not yet know where the journey will take us, we must nevertheless embark on it with courage and determination: as if it were a majestic march.

Music ends.

FLIGHT ATTENDANT. If you look out your window now you may see some beautiful landscapes of the German countryside. You may be able to see the woods

where Beethoven composed some of his best work.

A grand entrance of Beethoven and Schindler in a period carriage. Schindler enters first.

SCHINDLER. Early in May of 1822, the master traveled to the small village of Hetzendorf where he rented a beautiful house surrounded by a lovely park. He spent the summer there composing and going for very long walks in the countryside he loved so much.

BEETHOVEN. *(Taking in the country view.)* Look.

Schindler, look.

SCHINDLER. Yes, master.

BEETHOVEN. Do you see?

SCHINDLER. Yes. No. What?

BEETHOVEN. The countryside.

Here the sun is not concealed by any dirty roof. Here my senses can feast upon the spectacle of nature.

Smell.

Schindler does. It smells terrible.

SCHINDLER. Cow manure?

BEETHOVEN. Exactly!

Anything's better than the stench of Vienna and the Viennese.

My decree is to remain in the countryside. My miserable hearing does not plague me here.

We could return in the winter.

SCHINDLER. We have the rent at home to consider.

BEETHOVEN. Surely it will not be expensive to rent a lodging at that time of year.

Schindler, listen.

SCHINDLER. What?

BEETHOVEN. The sweet silence of the woods!

Beethoven begins to write.

SCHINDLER. The first composition he undertook there was the variations on Diabelli's waltz, which had taken his fancy in a curious way.

KATHERINE. *(Reading from the book.)* That phrase in Schindler's biography, "Diabelli's waltz had taken his fancy in a curious way."

SCHINDLER. Diabelli's waltz had taken his fancy in a curious way.

KATHERINE. What was curious about it? How had it taken his fancy? Schindler's biography doesn't elaborate on that.

SCHINDLER. *(Slightly annoyed with the interruption.)* In no time he had composed five variations, then five more, then two more. Every morning before dawn he was at his desk. The variations kept piling up and he kept saying:

BEETHOVEN. That is not all...there are more variations in here.

SCHINDLER. But master, Diabelli is concerned, lest the work should get too long and the publishing costs too high. He wants you to bring it to a close.

BEETHOVEN. Tell him to be patient yet a little longer.

SCHINDLER. Master, you should be working on the Mass, on the Ninth.

Why this trifle of a waltz? You've already composed twelve variations on it.

BEETHOVEN. Because there are more variations in here.

SCHINDLER. You're wasting your time.

Beethoven looks at him warningly. Schindler retracts.

I'm sorry. But I don't understand this obsession of yours.

Diabelli has said he doesn't need any more variations.

BEETHOVEN. I'm not making them for Mr. Diabolous.

SCHINDLER. You know he doesn't like it when you call him that.

Pause.

BEETHOVEN. Night and day I toil for the man. So, tell him to be patient yet a little longer. I am not done.

SCHINDLER. Fine.

FLIGHT ATTENDANT. In preparation for landing, please fasten your seatbelt. If you have been reading a book about Beethoven, we ask that you put it aside, return to the present and snap out of it. Welcome to the beautiful city of Bonn.

Projection: "Variation #7." We journey to Bonn, and a colorful overhead view of the city as seen in an old map. The pianist plays Variation #7.

Variation: "Bonn"

Beethoven appears at a table working in the background as Katherine enters; she has arrived in Bonn.

KATHERINE. Dear Clara,

I'm emailing you as requested.

Why must we always fight? Trust me when I tell you this is exactly where I am meant to be. Here I do not feel sick at all.

This city exudes music. Downtown is exactly as it was in the 1800s, except now there's a gigantic statue of Beethoven in the center of the main square. Imagine a town that doesn't have a military hero in their main square, but a musician. What great promise.

Last night I learned that their favorite local dish is pig's knuckles. Perhaps that's a part of the city's cultural life I'll have to do without.

I'm meeting Dr. Ladenburger tomorrow. At last, I get to see the sketchbooks. I can't wait.

Mom

P.S. How's *Hedda Gabler*?

Variation: "The Sketches—Part 1"

In the Beethoven-Haus, the home of the sketches.

The librarian, Dr. Gertie Ladenburger, eyes Katherine authoritatively, then guides Katherine to the archives.

GERTIE. *(Sternly.)* Dr. Kinderman must think highly of you. His recommendation is the only reason you're allowed in here.

KATHERINE. Well, it took me over a year to convince him.

GERTIE. Only a handful of people are permitted entrance to our archives. It's the most important collection in the world.

KATHERINE. I know. Thank you. That's why I'm here.

GERTIE. Your thesis…I'm not sure if our material can be of assistance in your search.

KATHERINE. Why not?

GERTIE. You are trying to find out why Beethoven became obsessed with Diabelli's waltz. It's really a question of inspiration. I do not think our sketches will help you with that.

KATHERINE. I guess I won't know until I look at them, will I?

Pause.

GERTIE. During your visit I will be with you whenever you're in the library. And I will give you a schedule of when you can come.

KATHERINE. Of course.

GERTIE. Come this way.

They get in the elevator, which goes down.

The entrance to the archives is in the sub-basement, four floors below *us*.

They arrive at the sub-basement.

Watch your step. Ah, here we are.

As the doors of the elevator open, we see an impressive sight: a multitude of towering shelves filled with sketchbooks and books. It looks like they go on forever. All catalogued and labeled.

After his death, Beethoven's sketchbooks were torn apart by autograph collectors and souvenir hunters so that hardly any book remained complete. These sketches are the survivors.

These sketches are the most intimate diary of his compositional process.

Many believe they are more important than the finished works, because they are closer to the original inspiration of the artist. You see, after an artist is done polishing a work, the initial instinct is marred by technique. These sketches show an unadulterated first impulse.

Pause.

But you wanted to see the sketches for the *Diabelli Variations, ja?*

KATHERINE. Yes.

Gertie goes to find it in the shelves.

GERTIE. Ah. Here we are.

She starts crossing to the library table to place the book.

Many of the sketches for the *Diab*...

Gertie and Beethoven cross paths. Gertie pauses a moment, shivers, is it possible she's perceived Beethoven's presence? No. Can't be. She continues to the table to place the book.

Many of the sketches for the *Diabelli Variations* are in this sketchbook.

She hands Katherine a pair of gloves.

Always wear gloves when touching the books. The oil in the fingers can damage the old paper. Are you ready?

KATHERINE. Yes.

GERTIE. Here we go.

Gertie opens the box. Projection: the image of the Wittgenstein Sketchbook cover. Gertie pulls the sketchbook out of its box.

This is the Wittgenstein Sketchbook.

In its present condition, it consists of forty-three leaves of "Honig" paper. The binding itself makes use of five stitch-holes.

This is the first page.

Gertie opens the book. A projection of the first page appears projected on the screen.

In this page you see who owned it.

After Beethoven died they auctioned his sketchbooks.

This one was bought and sold many times over the next hundred and thirty years. The composer Mendelssohn owned it. And the family of the philosopher Wittgenstein, which is how it got its name.

Gertie turns the page. Projection: the first page of Beethoven's sketches in his own handwriting appear.

Und this is the second page. These lines were made in this book almost two hundred years ago. He wrote first in pencil, and when he was sure, he went back over it with ink and highlighted the parts he liked.

And now, with this button, we get the infrared light.

Projection of a specially-lit sketch with blue and white effects.

You see how it turns blue? The bright white is the ink. These are the parts he chose to keep in the piece. The rest are ideas he discarded.

KATHERINE. Yes. I see.

GERTIE. This document records his compositional decisions.

Gertie turns the page. A projection of a full page of a sketch appears.

Some of these phrases have never been played before.

Here, this one has never been recorded. Look here.

Projection: We see the phrase of music in Beethoven's handwriting. It is a zoomed-in portion of a sketch for Variation #12. Over music:

You are hearing an original composition of Beethoven never before heard, except by the people who have read this book!

The pianist plays the phrase that's never been heard before.

KATHERINE. Indeed.

GERTIE. And here is what you're looking for.

Gertie turns the page. A projection of a sketch of Variation #3.

These are some of the sketches for the *Diabelli Variations.*

Katherine looks. She and Gertie examine the sketches. Clara and Mike appear. A phone conversation.

CLARA. Nurse Mike.

MIKE. Yes.

CLARA. This is Clara, Katherine Brandt's daughter. I hope it's OK I'm calling you on your cell phone.

MIKE. Of course.

CLARA. I'm sorry to bother you again, but it's just I'm very confused and I wanted to ask you… I got an email from my mother yesterday filled with typos.

MIKE. OK—

CLARA. You don't understand, my mother doesn't make typos. She just doesn't.

MIKE. I understand.

CLARA. I'm trying to read up and teach myself.

And I've been calling several doctors to get more information, and they all say the same thing: "Stay the course. Stay the course." What course?

There are no medicines, no treatment, no nothing.

Am I missing something?

MIKE. They can't tell you anything because we don't have anything. It's an orphan disease.

CLARA. A what?

MIKE. There are not enough patients to interest the pharmaceutical companies into producing medications. So there are no drugs coming down the pipeline. There is no pipeline.

CLARA. So eventually she won't be able to speak anymore.

MIKE. Not necessarily.

CLARA. And to top it all off, she's in BONN.

MIKE. Listen, I hope this isn't weird or anything, but would you want to meet and get something to eat?

CLARA. *(With trepidation.)* Oh.

Is he asking her out? Pause.

MIKE. So we can talk about your mother, and the illness, and…

CLARA. Oh, OK. That would be very helpful, thank you.

MIKE. OK, good. So I'll call you with the details.

CLARA. OK.

MIKE. Bye-bye.

CLARA. Bye.

Mike and Clara exit. We're back with Katherine and Gertie in the library.

KATHERINE. I can't decipher much of his handwriting.

GERTIE. Yes. It's hard to read. What are you looking for?

KATHERINE. I am looking for Diabelli's waltz.

Searches—Gertie turns the page. Projection: sketch of Variation #3.

Ah, here it is.

GERTIE. Yes, that's it.

Look, the first four bars.

Gertie points to it. Projection: zoomed in view of the first four bars of "Theme." The pianist plays it.

And here you can see all the sketches he made before he arrived at this variation.

Projection: initial sketch of Variation #3.

This is the first sketch he made.

Pianist plays sketch version 1. Projection highlights version 1 on the projected sketch.

Not satisfied with that, he made this.

Pianist plays sketch version 2. Projection highlights version 2.

And then this.

Pianist plays sketch version 3. Projection highlights version 3. Gertie turns the page.

And here's the variation itself.

The pianist plays Variation #3. Projection of final sketch of Variation #3.

KATHERINE. *(Over the music.)* I feel like I'm looking over his shoulder as he's composing.

GERTIE. *(Excited.)* Exactly. That's how I feel.

Gertie becomes embarassed at her sudden display of emotion, and exits.

KATHERINE. Dear Clara,

I have been here a little over a week. I am making such progress. Today I looked at the sketches for Variation number three; it's a waltz.

Diabelli's waltz is clumsy, repetitive.

But Beethoven's waltz is so light. So melodious.

Beethoven begins the variation on such a light note.

But here is the most interesting thing:

These three notes C, A, B-flat.

Repeated over and over.

He's pausing to think.

A lesser composer would have erased that passage, or changed those bars, but not him.

He wants you to see his moment of trepidation, of doubt.

And then he goes on, the notes ascending, ascending—a rising promise.

Music ends. Projection: a sketch with a food stain. Gertie reenters.

Dr. Ladenburger, What's this?

GERTIE. Some kind of food stain.

KATHERINE. It looks like wine.

GERTIE. *Nein.* It's probably soup. He loved soup.

Beethoven enters with a bowl in his hand.

BEETHOVEN. This soup is terrible. Frau Schnapps, what are you giving me?

Schindler. You said this soup is good. Does no one in this household know how to differentiate a tasty bowl of soup from a putrid, fetid, rancid, rotting pig's trough of stinking swill? Does no one have a palate in this house? Do I live amongst palateless people?

He exits.

KATHERINE. I didn't know he loved soup.

GERTIE. I didn't either, until I found soup in many of the sketches.

Katherine laughs.

These diaries are not only a record of his compositional process, they are also a record of his daily diet.

Katherine laughs.

Do you like pig's knees?

KATHERINE. I beg your pardon?

GERTIE. Pig's knees. It's Bonn's delicatessen. We are known all over Europe for our pig's knees.

KATHERINE. Pig's knuckles.

GERTIE. Ah *ja*, pig knuckles, you must try it.

KATHERINE. I don't eat much meat.

GERTIE. Good. You will like it.

Gertie and Katherine exit. Projection: "Variation #8." The pianist plays Variation #8.

Variation: "Classical Music"

Clara and Mike are at a concert sitting side by side facing forward. First date. They're both very nervous.

The pianist plays Variation #8.

We hear their inner monologues over the music. First Clara's, then Mike's.

CLARA. Maybe this wasn't such a good idea.

I almost said no. But I felt bad, he already had the tickets. And he's been so good about Mom.

She looks at him and he looks at her, they grin at each other. Their teeth showing a bit too long.

We're both so uncomfortable.
He probably hates this music.
He said he would teach me some physiotherapy for Mom. He has very pretty eyes.
I can hear him breathing. I wonder if he snores.

He crosses his arms and then puts them on his knees.

He smells good.

Mike's hand slowly drifts toward her.

Oh the hand, what, what's with the hand?…

Mike draws his hand back.

Oh, that was awkward.
There was too much garlic in that pasta, I wish I had a mint.
I'm not very good at this.

He holds her hand.

OK. OK. OK. Just go with it.

She takes a deep breath. Pause. Blackout. Music ends. Projection: "Variation #8". Lights up. The pianist plays Variation #8 again. Same scene but now the light is slightly brighter on Mike.

MIKE. *(Over the music.)* G_d, I wish I knew more about what I'm listening to. It all sounds like "classical" music to me.

I hope she likes it.
Is she looking at me?

She looks at him and he looks at her, they smile at each other. This is the same moment we witnessed before.

What kind of face is this? I feel like I pulled a muscle.

He reaches to take Clara's hand, changes his mind, and instead crosses his arms.

Maybe not

He then puts them on his knees.

That was awkward.
What am I doing with my hands?
She smells so good.
OK, now hold her hand.

He looks over at her and doesn't.

Hold her hand. Hold her hand! Hold her hand!

He does.

That was subtle!
Oh my G_d, she's holding it back.
Best. Concert. Ever.

Music ends. Lights change.

Variation: "Sketches—Part 2"

The pianist plays Variation #13.

It's a very farcical variation, reminiscent of the chase-scene music in silent films. Schindler appears out of breath as he's being chased by Diabelli, who's trying to get an answer from him as to when the variations will be ready. During the music a chase sequence is reenacted between them. As the music ends, Diabelli finally catches Schindler and says:

DIABELLI. Schindler, please. It's been almost a year.
I need to publish these variations. My firm needs to publish these variations.

SCHINDLER. He is not happy with them yet.

DIABELLI. What do you mean he's not happy with them?

SCHINDLER. He won't let you publish them yet. He's not finished.

DIABELLI. But Schindler…

Beethoven enters abruptly, then sees Diabelli and tries to flee. Too late.

Maestro! Thank G_d! I must speak with you.

Beethoven gestures to his throat, mouthing words silently, pretending his throat's sore.

What? What?

Diabelli looks at Schindler.

What?

SCHINDLER. Uhhh...yes, the master has a very sore throat and can't speak.

Beethoven tries to leave.

DIABELLI. Maestro, wait!

Beethoven stops.

When will the work be ready? Just give me a date.

I think nineteen variations is enough. We don't need more. I can't publish more.

Beethoven writes in a book.

(Trying to read it.) I can't decipher his writing.

SCHINDLER. *(Reading.)* He says he can't give you a date.

DIABELLI. *(To Schindler.)* Why not? *(Then to Beethoven.)* Why not?

Beethoven writes briefly.

SCHINDLER. The master says he can't control how many variations there are. The beautiful theme you've composed is the only thing that will determine how many exist in it.

When the theme is exhausted, the master will stop.

DIABELLI. He wrote all that?

SCHINDLER. He writes very fast.

DIABELLI. Very. *(To Beethoven.)* I need it for the publishing house. We have sold almost nothing this year. I don't want to go back to teaching twelve-year-olds the guitar.

Beethoven writes.

SCHINDLER. He asks if you've tried selling wine. He says more people like wine.

DIABELLI. You mustn't mock me.

I served you well while I was working at Steiner. I was always at your disposal. I don't understand why he's behaving this way.

BEETHOVEN. Diabelli, I am making it better.

Beethoven exits.

DIABELLI. Maestro!

SCHINDLER. Pardon me. I must tend to the master.

Schindler exits. Diabelli makes sure everyone's gone and crosses over to the table where the sketches are. Carefully he picks one up. Then another. He begins to read the sketches.

Variation: "Baseball"

Sound of a train passing. Gertie sits on a bench in a train station, reading. Katherine enters. She notices Gertie.

KATHERINE. Oh, hello. I didn't know you used this station.

GERTIE. Yes.

Pause. Gertie goes back to reading.

KATHERINE. I want to thank you so much for your help with the sketches. It's been invaluable. I have learned so much these past three months.

GERTIE. Good.

Pause.

KATHERINE. It's a beautiful city.

GERTIE. Yes.

KATHERINE. Oh, I am sorry, you are reading.

GERTIE. No. It is OK.

KATHERINE. What are you reading?

GERTIE. A book on Mozart.

KATHERINE. Mozart? Don't you feel like you're cheating on Beethoven?

She laughs. No response from Gertie.

Seeing the sketches, I almost feel like…

Katherine gestures.

GERTIE. Yes, I remember when I first started that I had the same feelings.

She notices Katherine's hand.

You are in pain?

KATHERINE. No. No, I am not.

GERTIE. What is the problem with the hand?

KATHERINE. Oh, it's nothing, nothing.

GERTIE. I saw you in the library when you tried to pick up the book.

KATHERINE. *(Cutting her off.)* It's nothing.

GERTIE. You don't have to tell me.

KATHERINE. Do you follow baseball at all?

GERTIE. Do I look like a woman who follows baseball?

KATHERINE. Well, there was a player, Lou Gehrig. – Ah.

GERTIE. *(Nodding.)* Amyotrophic lateral sclerosis.

KATHERINE. How do you know that?

GERTIE. I thought that is what you had.
My aunt, five years ago we lost her.

Pause.

It's a waste…

KATHERINE. Excuse me?

GERTIE. This train is not coming. It's a waste of our time.

Variation: "Circus Music"

Schindler enters and finds Diabelli studying the sketches.

SCHINDLER. Diabelli! What are you doing in here? Are you mad?

DIABELLI. Look at this, Schindler. Look! He's mocking my waltz. He's mocking me!

SCHINDLER. Do you know what he would do to you if he found you touching his sketches?

DIABELLI. He's turned my waltz into a mad march.

The pianist plays Variation #1 and continues until the next variation is mentioned.

Like toy soldiers marching.

He can't do this. This is the first variation. The first variation must always follow the meter of the theme. He can't turn my waltz into a march. That's just not done. These are the rules!

SCHINDLER. You really expect Beethoven to conform to the musical conventions of the day?

Music ends.

DIABELLI. And look at this one.

Variation #21 plays.

It's like circus music. Look!

Clowns will dance to this music!

SCHINDLER. Diabelli, watch what you're saying.

Music ends.

DIABELLI. And here what's this—a fugue?!

Variation #30 plays rapidly.

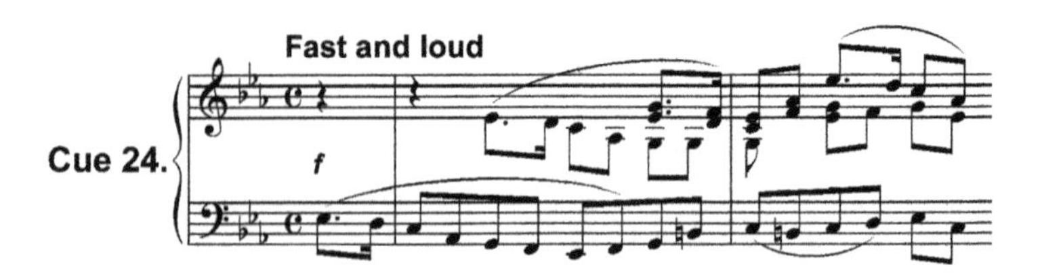

Everyone knows Beethoven can't write fugues. His fugues are terrible.

Music ends.

SCHINDLER. They are not terrible. They are just not very good.

DIABELLI. Schindler. His fugues are terrible!

Is this why he took on this commission, to mock me?

SCHINDLER. Diabelli, these are sketches. The master is trying things out. These are not the final variations. You can't judge from these. That would be like looking at a pencil sketch of the *Mona Lisa* and complaining about the color.

DIABELLI. But my waltz is so...my theme is so...

SCHINDLER. Diabelli, it is a testament to your composition that the master is finding so much in it.

DIABELLI. Schindler, please don't flatter me...

SCHINDLER. I am telling you the truth. Look at all the work he's putting into it.

He pulls out sketches.

And here's more.

Pulls more sketches out.

I keep urging him to work on the Mass or the Ninth, both more lucrative by far. But he's obsessed with your waltz.

DIABELLI. Really? So, these are all sketches for my variations?

SCHINDLER. Yes. He returns to it at all hours, day and night.

DIABELLI. He does?

SCHINDLER. You should be happy Beethoven is even looking at your insignificant waltz!

Pause.

DIABELLI. *(Shocked and hurt by this.)* You hate my waltz! You think it insignificant.

Schindler doesn't respond.

SCHINDLER. I'm sorry. I didn't mean to be so blunt. But you drive one to madness with your eternal nagging.

DIABELLI. Thank you. That makes me feel much better.
So if it's so insignificant, why is the master pursuing it?

SCHINDLER. It's baffling to me.

DIABELLI. Of course it's baffling to you. You aspire to the stuffy rooms of the palaces and the aristocracy.
You can't understand what I mean with my waltz.
But maybe your master can.

Variation: "Clara"

Back at the train station.

KATHERINE. I think Beethoven *is* making fun of Diabelli's waltz.

GERTIE. Making fun of it?

KATHERINE. Yes. There's so much humor in the variations.
He's mocking the waltz. Showing it for all its ineptitude. You can see that in so

many of his sketches.

GERTIE. So this is your hypothesis?

KATHERINE. Diabelli's waltz is ordinary and it's mediocre.

Beethoven will go on to show Vienna what a great composition he can make out of a grain of sand.

GERTIE. I'm not convinced.

Oh. I almost forgot. Your daughter called again.

KATHERINE. Thank you.

She puts the note in her bag without looking at it. Pause.

GERTIE. Are you upset with your daughter?

KATHERINE. No. Why?

GERTIE. Well, she calls you almost every day. And you don't call her back. Don't you like your daughter?

Katherine looks at Gertie.

I mean you love her, of course. But you don't like her, do you?

KATHERINE. My daughter is… I don't know how to explain it.

She's like her father. He was a good man, a good father, but he couldn't stick with anything and got mired in mediocrity. And I'm afraid she's like him.

First she was a sculptor, then she joined a band, then she was a painter. Now she's a costume designer, but she's about to change that too. And it's the same with the men in her life.

I fear she'll never truly be anything. I'm afraid my daughter is mediocre.

GERTIE. Hmmm.

KATHERINE. What?

GERTIE. Nothing.

Sound of train.

Here's our train.

Variation: "Dancing"

Mike and Clara enter dancing. They're at a nightclub. Music blares. Mike is doing some elaborate hip-hop steps. Clara is laughing at Mike's moves. They have a good time.

CLARA. *(Trying to yell over the music.)* It's really hot.

MIKE. Thank you. I'm taking classes.

CLARA. OK. Yeah. Also, it's hot in here.

MIKE. Oh, oh. Do you want to go outside?

CLARA. Yes. Thank you.

They move outside.

MIKE. Oh, it's so nice out.

CLARA. I love New York at this time of year. The air is so crisp.

MIKE. Are you having a good time?

CLARA. Yes, I love that song.

MIKE. You know who that is?

CLARA. *(Walking away coyly.)* Yeah. I actually used to play their music when I toured with my band.

MIKE. Oh wow. I never pictured you in a band.

Clara gives Mike a confused look.

Because you know so much about classical music.

CLARA. That's just because my mom started taking me to her music lectures when I was seven years old.

MIKE. You were doing a little graduate work when you were seven?

CLARA. Post grad.

After my dad died, we couldn't afford a babysitter, so I would go along to her lectures.

MIKE. *(Sarcastically.)* That sounds like fun.

CLARA. Actually it was. I loved watching my mother up there at the podium. And I loved watching the faces of her students. They were mesmerized. Most kids hate it when their parents work all the time, but I loved it because that's when she's at her best. And it kills me that when she looks at me all she sees is failure.

MIKE. *(Getting a newspaper clipping out of his pocket.)* If that's all she sees, your mom is blind. Or maybe she didn't see this.

CLARA. Oh, no!

MIKE. Oh, yes. "*Hedda Gabler* looked sumptuous and elegant in costumes designed by the very talented Ms. Clara Brandt." Congratulations!

CLARA. *(Blushing and smiling.)* Thank you very much. My mother is thrilled I got a rave review in the *Village Voice*.

MIKE. My parents are proud of me if I leave the house with pants on. What's the deal?

CLARA. I just don't want to do the same thing for twenty years! I love doing something for a few years, learning about it and moving on. For me that's a life better lived.

Mike yawns and uses the gesture to put his arm behind Clara.

Old school.

MIKE. That's how I roll.

Mike leans into Clara and then he kisses her gently on the lips. Then more passionately. She responds in kind, but then pulls away.

CLARA. No, stop.

MIKE. We've been doing this for three months.

CLARA. I know, I'm sorry.
I'm all over the place, and you, I really like you, and I have a great time with you.

MIKE. Then what is it?

CLARA. You're so nice…

MIKE. *(Play-acting as if he's been hit by a bullet in the stomach. Feigning great pain.)* Ouch!

CLARA. And, you're so great…

MIKE. *(Even more wounded.)* UGGH!

CLARA. No… My mom's health is deteriorating and it is only going to get worse. And I don't think you want to be around for it.

MIKE. I know better than you what I'm getting myself into. And I can help.

CLARA. I don't want your help. I don't want to be part of your caseload.

MIKE. You're not. Can't you tell I really like you?

CLARA. Don't say that.

MIKE. Why not?

CLARA. Things between my mother and me are really difficult, and I need to focus on that right now.

MIKE. OK. You do what you got to do.

CLARA. I'm sorry, I know. It's just, my mother fell in the library yesterday.

MIKE. Why didn't you tell me?

CLARA. She had to be hospitalized for a day.

Katherine enters on the other side of the stage.

KATHERINE. I am fine. I am OK. Just a little tired, that's all.

CLARA. *(To Mike.)* The hospital called me.

KATHERINE. Nothing to worry about. I tripped and fell. Must have been too focused on the work.

CLARA. Mom!

KATHERINE. Clara, every day I'm making new discoveries. With Dr. Landenberger's help, I may well be done sooner than expected.

CLARA. *(To Mike.)* That's what she said when I asked her about the episode.

KATHERINE. And how's Mark?

CLARA. His name is Mike.

KATHERINE. Sorry, Mike.

CLARA. He's fine.

KATHERINE. Mmm-hmm.

CLARA. What?

KATHERINE. It's just strange. You're dating a man who saw me naked.

CLARA. Yes, Mom. And oddly, that's all he talks about!

KATHERINE. Clara! I hope you are seeing other people too. Yes?

CLARA. Because he saw you naked?

KATHERINE. No. Because he's not right for you. You need someone who challenges you.

CLARA. Mom, why don't you come home?
Your doctors are here.

KATHERINE. I'm fine. It was nothing. And the university is threatening to cut my grant in half.
They're worried they're not getting their money's worth. I have to stay here.

CLARA. No! You are not fine.

KATHERINE. Thank you.

CLARA. You're ill and you're putting yourself in danger.

Pause.

Mom.

KATHERINE. I'm here.

Pause.

CLARA. Listen.
I was thinking of taking a vacation. I was thinking of going to Europe.
Maybe I can stop by and visit with you.

KATHERINE. Absolutely not.

CLARA. Why not?

KATHERINE. It's not the right time.

CLARA. I want to spend some time with you before I have to be your nurse!

MIKE. You said that to her?

CLARA. Yep.

MIKE. And what did she say?

CLARA. She hung up.

Variation: "Accidents of Fate"

Beethoven walks in from the outside. He's upset. Schindler follows him.

BEETHOVEN. What? What? What? Out with it! You've been sulking the whole way home. Just say it.

Schindler looks at Beethoven accusingly but says nothing.

Those people want the music I make, but they don't understand what it takes to

make it. I had an idea. I needed to get to the carriage to write down the idea so I could make it into something!

Schindler is silent. He hangs Beethoven's coat up.

Speak.

SCHINDLER. How will you pay your rent this month?

BEETHOVEN. You'll figure something out.

SCHINDLER. If you had just tipped your hat to the count, he would have given us a commission.

BEETHOVEN. He wanted to talk to me! That's an hour of my time. That count doesn't hold a conversation! He is like a woodpecker attached to a gargantuan tree hammering on the hollow trunk for hours! I need to find an ending to the variations.

SCHINDLER. You may be evicted. Would it have been so difficult for you to stop and greet him the way one ought to greet a count?

BEETHOVEN. I was thinking! I didn't notice him!

SCHINDLER. Master, everyone saw you pull your hat down below your eyes and ignore him.

Beethoven laughs to himself.

You think that's funny?

A ringing, distorted sound effect representing Beethoven's hearing problems occurs during Schindler's line.

The count was humiliated in front of all his friends! They were all shocked by your behavior.

BEETHOVEN. If I show respect for a person, it will be because that person earned my respect with his deeds. Not because of his title.

SCHINDLER. I think that's wonderful.

I'll tell that to the landlord when he comes for the rent.

BEETHOVEN. They want me to be a dancing monkey in their courts.

The counts, the countesses, the dukes and duchesses, the barons and baronesses, there are thousands of them. There's only one Beethoven!

No wonder their heads are rolling all over Europe.

SCHINDLER. Master! Please, you mustn't say such things! Schubert was arrested yesterday for saying much less.

BEETHOVEN. Let them arrest me! Did you hear that the government has decreed that people cannot dance the waltz? I will not bow down to this paralytic regime.

Ringing sound returns. It hurts even more.

Pause.

SCHINDLER. Master, your ears are bothering you, aren't they? Is it the ringing?

BEETHOVEN. That's not important.

He shows him his sketchpad.

This is what I was thinking about when that man started talking to me.

Schindler walks away.

SCHINDLER. It's not important what you—

BEETHOVEN. Would you please come and see this?
Here's the first trill in Diabelli's waltz, yes?

Trill plays.

Cue 25.

SCHINDLER. Yes.

BEETHOVEN. Now look at what I've done. I've taken these four notes *(Played slowly.)* and used them in this variation.

Beethoven shows Schindler different sketches he's been working on. The pianist plays part of Variation #11.

And in this one.

The pianist plays part of Variation #16.

And in this one.

The pianist plays part of Variation #6 and continues to end of scene.

And that's all with four notes. Now, you can have that music, or you can have me talking with the count.

Ringing, distorted sound occurs again, but louder. Music fades. Beethoven holds his ears. The pain is great; the loud ringing sound tormenting. Then, the pianist plays Variation #20.

Variation: "The Exam"

As Variation #20 continues to play, projection: "Variation #20."

Katherine enters the examination room. She takes off her jacket, her blouse and her bra. She sets them carefully on the gurney.

She then sits on the gurney and faces downstage.

She sits up straight and the lights go out. We see an X-ray being taken. Every time an X-ray is taken we hear the loud thump of the machine.

The room is in complete darkness. The only light in the scene is what would be the light from the X-rays (or a theatrical version of that, so that every time an X-ray is taken, a square of light is shone on Katherine's naked body. It makes for a sort of slow strobe-light effect.

The session begins:

> *Two X-rays are taken of her facing front.*
>
> *Two X-rays are taken of her facing right.*
>
> *Two X-rays are taken of her facing left.*
>
> *Then she turns front again.*

More X-rays. Slowly at first. Then progressively faster. More oppressive. It is almost as if the machine is torturing Katherine. This is how she's perceiving this battery of tests.

As this progresses, Katherine gets more and more upset by the way this brutal sound bruises her.

It's the first time we see the depth of her sadness.

She realizes how naked she is and tries to cover herself. A futile gesture considering the circumstances. The futility of it all makes her more upset. She sobs quietly.

Into this room, Beethoven enters slowly, in his own world—looking at some sketches, perhaps. He crosses behind her, then sits on the gurney right behind Katherine but facing upstage.

Without acknowledging that Beethoven just sat down on the gurney behind her, Katherine slowly leans back until she finds his back and leans on him, her head resting on his back…

She finds a modicum of peace and comfort in the subject of her obsession. Blackout.

Variation: "Septet"

Projection: A collection of X-ray images—the result of Katherine's tests are projected on the stage. Mike enters with Clara.

CLARA. So?

MIKE. *(Examining Katherine's chart.)* Well, nothing's broken. So that's good.

CLARA. But…

MIKE. Well, they tried to find out why she fell, they did a number of tests. The results are mixed.

CLARA. Just tell me.

MIKE. Her forced vital capacity has been reduced by thirty-nine percent and her muscle elasticity and strength by thirty-four percent.

CLARA. In English?

MIKE. She has to start using a walker or she's gonna hurt herself.

CLARA. OK…

MIKE. And she might need a wheelchair soon.

CLARA. So the entire schedule they gave me has been a lie.

Katherine enters using a cane. Gertie follows.

GERTIE. So what's the result?

KATHERINE. My doctors are not very optimistic.

CLARA. They said she would walk for at least a couple more years.
It's been seven months.

GERTIE. So how long?

KATHERINE. It's hard to tell. It could plateau and I could stay like this for a while.

CLARA. I want to know how long she has.

MIKE. It's hard to tell.

CLARA. Just tell me!

MIKE. A year. Maybe a year and a half.

GERTIE. So are you going home?

KATHERINE. Absolutely not.

CLARA. I have to bring her home.

KATHERINE. I must stay here.

MIKE. She doesn't want to come home. She's told you that.

CLARA. I don't care.

GERTIE. Are you sure?

KATHERINE. Yes. I'm staying here.

MIKE. If I was in your family, I'd want to be with you all the time.

CLARA. Please don't say that.

Beethoven enters followed by Schindler.

SCHINDLER. Master! Please don't say that.

BEETHOVEN. I can't do it. I can't do it.

SCHINDLER. Master, calm down.

CLARA. Mike, this is not the time.

KATHERINE and BEETHOVEN. I need more time.

MIKE. Then you should GO.

GERTIE. Then you should stay.

CLARA and KATHERINE. My mother/daughter will kill me.

MIKE and GERTIE. Sometimes you have to be selfish.

BEETHOVEN. I can't finish these variations. I don't know how to finish the set.

MIKE. I want to come with you.

GERTIE. I can be of help.

SCHINDLER. Diabelli will come for you.

KATHERINE and CLARA. Thank you.

CLARA. Thank you, but no. I need to go alone.

BEETHOVEN. I need to be alone.

MIKE. Why?

CLARA. Because we barely know each other. That kind of pressure could kill whatever this is.

MIKE. So there is a this.

CLARA and BEETHOVEN. *(Exasperated.)* Ahh—

GERTIE. I learned a few things with my aunt so I can be of help.

KATHERINE. I might need some help.

MIKE. You're going to need help.

SCHINDLER. Master, how can I help?

BEETHOVEN. You can't help. I can't find an ending for the set.

DIABELLI. *(Entering.)* What do you mean, he can't find an ending?

CLARA, SCHINDLER, and BEETHOVEN. It's all wrong.

BEETHOVEN. The composition has run away without me and I don't know how to end it.

DIABELLI. Does he know what he is doing to me?

MIKE. You'll need someone who knows what they're doing.

CLARA. We would have to leave now.

GERTIE and MIKE. You have to slow down.

KATHERINE, CLARA, and BEETHOVEN. Time is scarce.

The pianist begins to play softly underneath the following text to the end of the Act:

DIABELLI and CLARA. I can't wait any longer.

BEETHOVEN and KATHERINE. I have so much to do.

SCHINDLER, MIKE, GERTIE, and DIABELLI. Please.

CLARA. How do I convince her?

MIKE. Listen to me.

MIKE and GERTIE. You have an opportunity here.

BEETHOVEN. I must not lose this opportunity.

KATHERINE. This is my last opportunity.

CLARA. This is my last opportunity.

During the following, when a (/) is indicated, it means the following character's first word overlaps with the word directly before the (/).

MIKE. I can help (/). Let me help. Time is scarce. Let me help.

CLARA. Time is scarce (/). I can't wait. I have to go now. Time is scarce.

SCHINDLER. Let me help (/). Time is scarce. I can help. Time is scarce.

DIABELLI. Time is scarce (/). I can't wait any longer. Time is scarce.

GERTIE. I can help. You should stay. Help.

BEETHOVEN and KATHERINE. I must have the chance to finish the work.

During this final cacophony, the music builds in volume with the actors, and after the last line, the pianist plays this:

End of Act One

ACT TWO

Variation: "Here Be Dragons"

Darkness. Projection: "Variation #19." The pianist plays Variation #19.

A light comes up on Katherine. She is using a walker. At various intervals Clara, Mike, Gertie, Schindler, and Diabelli enter. Onstage, all times and places come together. Clara and Mike carry suitcases, having just arrived in Bonn. Gertie is in the library, while Schindler carries a bowl

and washcloth for tending to Beethoven. Diabelli enters and looks at his pocketwatch. His clothing is much more expensive and ostentatious than in Act One.

KATHERINE. *(To the audience.)* Transfiguration is an interesting idea.

Not the Christian idea of Jesus on the mountain and His face changing all of a sudden and being filled with light and John and Peter and that other guy being surprised by it.

No. Not that transfiguration. I'm not religious so…no.

But the IDEA of transfiguration. Transforming one thing into something better. Moving from the banal to the exalted.

What if Beethoven is transfiguring Diabelli's waltz?

If that is the case, the large set of variations is not an exercise in making something out of nothing as I had previously thought. But instead, a study in transfiguring the waltz into its better self.

Pause.

But not all things transfigure into their better selves. No. *(Referring to herself.)* My motor neurons are deteriorating rapidly, every day my muscles are receiving fewer and fewer signals from my brain, so they are atrophying.

But the best part of this is that my brain remains untouched by the illness! So that I am able to fully experience the process by which my body is becoming but a flaccid carcass.

Transfiguration indeed.

My daughter arrived in Bonn two weeks ago. She's trying to help.

Perhaps children ought to be the way in which we transfigure. The way we become our better selves.

Clara was always piercingly observant and original in her thinking.

When she was a child, she asked me one day, "Mom, does G_d sing songs?"

I was intrigued by the question. Why do you ask that?

"Because," she replied, "when you listen to music, Mom, you look like you're talking with G_d."

She was seven years old.

She smiles.

Observant indeed. But she meanders through life. She experiences everything but commits to nothing.

Children! HERE BE DRAGONS!

Katherine crosses away and Clara takes center stage.

CLARA. We have been in Bonn two weeks.

Seventeenth-century houses collide with Cold War buildings to create a landscape where both feel out of place.

I came to bring her home, but, well… You know how that went.

She has gotten worse: much worse than she let on in any of our telephone conversations.

She was very upset I came. And even more upset Mike came with me.

But in these two weeks we've begun to fall into a routine of sorts.

My mother goes to the archive. Mike has a part-time gig at the Red Cross. I am volunteering in the scenic shop at a local theatre. I do the shopping for the house and at night we all eat together.

But like the buildings in this city, we all feel out of place. As my mother would say: "HERE BE DRAGONS."

English mapmakers in the sixteenth century placed the phrase "here be dragons" at the edges of their known world.

They meant to imply that a) well, there were dragons there, and b) that venturing into those regions was a risky proposition.

Lights change. Sound of thunder and rain. Diabelli hurries onstage and is met by Schindler.

Variation: "The Conversation Notebooks"

This scene shifts between the two time periods seamlessly, with no scenery changes. One is Beethoven's apartment where Diabelli and Schindler meet, the other is the archives where Katherine and Gertie are working.

DIABELLI. *(Entering in a hurry.)* I came as soon as I heard.

SCHINDLER. Good afternoon, Anton.

DIABELLI. How is he?

SCHINDLER. He's better now.

DIABELLI. Thank G_d.

SCHINDLER. We almost lost him. But he's come through.

DIABELLI. Oh, poor man.

On the opposite side of the stage.

GERTIE. So there are no sketches for the variations between 1819 and 1822?

KATHERINE. I haven't found any.

GERTIE. Did you check all the stacks?

KATHERINE. Yes.

GERTIE. So he stopped working on the variations for three years?

KATHERINE. It seems that way.

SCHINDLER. It came over him suddenly. The coughing was terrible, but the doctors bled him and they say he's out of danger.

DIABELLI. This after a year of jaundice!

SCHINDLER. Indeed. Do you wish to see him?

DIABELLI. Yes, please.

Schindler hands Diabelli a conversation notebook.

What is this?

SCHINDLER. Our friend is completely deaf now. So you must write down what you wish to say to him.

DIABELLI. And does he write back?

SCHINDLER. No. He will speak back to you.

DIABELLI. I understand.

They enter Beethoven's room. Diabelli is shocked when he sees the composer. He looks so close to death. Because the conversation books don't record Beethoven's replies, Beethoven is not there. In the following exchange Diabelli speaks into the audience and we are forced to imagine what Beethoven replied.

How are you, maestro? You look well.

Beethoven responded something here. To which Diabelli said:

No. Luigi. You do look well.

Beethoven replies.

GERTIE. But what we do have is the conversation book of November 1822.

Gertie takes the conversation book from Diabelli's hands.

DIABELLI. All of Vienna is praying for your quick recovery.

Beethoven replies.

You can't blame them for wanting your music.

KATHERINE. *(Reading.)* You can't blame them for wanting your music.

GERTIE. We don't know how Beethoven responded.

DIABELLI. Everyone's eager to hear your Mass. All of Vienna is talking about it.

Beethoven replies.

It is? When can we hear it?

Beethoven replies.

That's wonderful. No one can believe all you've accomplished during your illness.

KATHERINE. Beethoven exists in the silences.

DIABELLI. Anyone else would have given up. But not you.

Beethoven replies.

Yes. We are prepared. As soon as you give us the Mass, we'll publish it.

Beethoven replies.

We all eagerly await the chance to hear it.

SCHINDLER. Anton, we should let him sleep.

DIABELLI. *(To Schindler.)* Yes. *(To Beethoven.)* Luigi, we are all praying for your recovery. Goodbye.

KATHERINE. He was very ill for those three years. Many times on the brink of death.

GERTIE. An appropriate time to write a Mass.

Schindler helps Diabelli with his coat.

DIABELLI. He says the Mass is nearly finished?

SCHINDLER. It is.

DIABELLI. Wonderful.

SCHINDLER. I think he's on his way to recovery.

DIABELLI. What makes you say that?

SCHINDLER. Today he fired the cook.

Diabelli laughs.

He also said that from now on he would endeavor to surpass everything he's ever done before.

DIABELLI. If there's someone who can do it.

SCHINDLER. He seems to be on his way—the new symphony will have a choir in it.

DIABELLI. A choir?

SCHINDLER. And he's writing a sonata in two parts.

DIABELLI. I can't wait to hear them.

GERTIE. I think you are right. Diabelli seems to have given up on getting the variations.

KATHERINE. His company is doing very well. He's a wealthy man now.
And he is getting the Mass—a much more important work from Beethoven.

DIABELLI. Please take care of him. He looks much worse than I thought.

SCHINDLER. I'll do my best.

Schindler and Diabelli exit. The pianist plays the introduction of Variation #26.

Variation: "Physical Therapy"

Projection: "Variation #26."

Mike is doing physiotherapy with Katherine. She sits. He grabs her left arm and raises it back and forth to improve elasticity. Clara watches from a distance. Katherine is obviously uncomfortable with these two uninvited guests in her apartment.

MIKE. This is helping with elasticity and slowing down the calcification of the joints. You want to keep flexible.

KATHERINE. I need to get back to the archives.

MIKE. *(Continuing the physiotherapy.)* Just a bit longer.
Clara, you should learn how to do this.

CLARA. *(Equally uncomfortable with the whole thing.)* Yes. I'm watching.

MIKE. Why don't you take your mother's arm and I'll show you.

Katherine and Clara look at each other, neither wants to touch the other.

KATHERINE and CLARA. No. That's not…

KATHERINE. I'll get a nurse to do it. You don't have to learn to do this.

CLARA. You sure? I can do it.

KATHERINE. *(To Clara.)* It's fine. *(To Mike.)* Mike, she can watch.

MIKE. No! It's important she understand how to do this when I am not here. It will help with the pain.

KATHERINE. Is this really necessary?

MIKE. It is.
Come, take your mother's arm.

After a moment's hesitation, Clara approaches Katherine and takes her arm. Touching is not something these two women do often. Clara begins to imitate the movements Mike is doing. The whole thing is very awkward for both women.

Is that OK?

KATHERINE. Yes!

MIKE. If anything feels uncomfortable or you have pain at any time, let me know.
We're just going to move the shoulder first. In and out.

Mike and Clara move Katherine's arms across her chest and then back out to the sides of her body. Katherine flinches in pain.

KATHERINE. Ow.

Clara puts her mother's arm down.

CLARA. I'm hurting her.

KATHERINE. It's OK. It's not you. It's just a bit stiff.

MIKE. Here.

Mike crosses to the other side of Katherine, and guides Clara.

Let me help you. Let's try it again.

Breathe in, Dr. Brandt, breathe out.

Clara continues moving her mother's arm.

Breathe in, breathe out.

The pianist plays Variation #26 as the exercises continue.

That's good, Clara.

Slowly, almost imperceptibly, mother and daughter are breathing together.

This simple act of physiotherapy has created a momentary truce.

Now do you feel it in your chest? Do you feel it opening up?

KATHERINE. Yes.

Mike crosses back to his original position beside Katherine and takes her other arm.

MIKE. OK.

Clara and Mike move Katherine's arms in and out with each breath. All three move in unison for a moment. It becomes a sort of dance.

Big breath in.
And we breathe with her.
Big breath out.
And in, and out.
And now I'm going to bring her arm up.

Mike raises Katherine's arm above her head. Clara follows suit.

KATHERINE. What should I do?

MIKE. Nothing.
Your job right now is to...submit to my command.

Katherine gives Mike a look that reminds him she has no sense of humor. Mike and Clara move Katherine's arms with the music.

Keep breathing, Dr. Brandt.
OK, let's try to stand. It'll be good for your leg muscles.

KATHERINE. Be careful.

MIKE. We'll help you. Clara, will you hold her under the arm?

Clara and Mike hoist Katherine to her feet.

KATHERINE. Oh, hello, world.

MIKE. Hello.

CLARA. *(With a funny voice to make her mother laugh.)* Hola.

Katherine begins to laugh and cannot stop. The pianist stops playing Variation #26.

It wasn't that funny.

MIKE. Let's sit her down.

Mike and Clara return Katherine to her chair. She's still laughing uncontrollably.

CLARA. What's going on?

MIKE. It's a symptom.

CLARA. Laughing?

MIKE. It's called emotional incontinence.

Katherine's amplified laughter continues.

Variation: "Joyful Silence"

Beethoven enters. He looks twenty years older. We hear his breathing as if we were inside his head. He is composing. He crosses downstage, deep in thought. We hear only his breathing. But then, the notes begin to appear projected on the upstage screen one by one as if Beethoven was writing them. We are witnessing Beethoven compose. Schindler enters.

SCHINDLER. I arrived at six o'clock in the evening at the master's house. Whereupon, I learned that there had been a quarrel after midnight and that both maids had run away. They had waited too long to bring the master his dinner, and when they finally did, it was ruined. As I entered the house, I heard the master singing in the parlor behind a closed door—not singing, howling. Stamping. After listening for a long time to this scene, I was about to go when the door flew open.

BEETHOVEN. Look! Look what they've done to me. Everyone has run away and I haven't had anything to eat since yesterday.

It's all your fault.

SCHINDLER. You fired me.

BEETHOVEN. That's your excuse?

SCHINDLER. *(Noticing the shutters.)* Master, what did you do to the shutters?

BEETHOVEN. What are you saying? You have to look at me. I can't read your lips if you're not looking at me.

SCHINDLER. *(Looking at Beethoven.)* What did you do to the shutters? You wrote on the shutters, they are all filled with your writing.

BEETHOVEN. I ran out of paper.

SCHINDLER. They are ruined. You will be evicted again. That'll be the third move in a month.

BEETHOVEN. Don't you see? After three years, the waltz still has so much to offer me.

SCHINDLER. What waltz?

BEETHOVEN. Diabelli's waltz.

SCHINDLER. I thought you had given up on it?

BEETHOVEN. *(Defensive.)* I never gave up on it, I just couldn't find an ending.

SCHINDLER. So you have an ending now?

BEETHOVEN. No! But I picked up the waltz and discovered that it still has so much more to offer me. There is still more life in this waltz. That's why I couldn't find an ending. It's not yet time for an ending. Look, six shutters full.

SCHINDLER. This is all from Diabelli's waltz?

BEETHOVEN. Yes.

SCHINDLER. *(Looking at the shutters.)* I don't understand this.

BEETHOVEN. These are new forms. It is impossible to express new ideas using old forms. These are new forms.

When I am done with this set of variations, I will have revolutionized what we now understand to be variation form.

SCHINDLER. Which means Diabelli won't sell a single copy.

BEETHOVEN. *(Playfully delighted.)* That's exactly what it means.

SCHINDLER. I can't wait to tell him.

Pause.

Master, you're famished. Come, we'll find you something to eat.

Schindler gently guides Beethoven offstage, while Beethoven's gaze remains on the shutters. The pianist plays Variation #26 in the transition.

Variation: "The Discovery"

Gertie is at the table in the library looking at the books and sketches. Katherine enters with a walker.

GERTIE. I am looking, but I don't see it here. Did you check upstairs?

KATHERINE. I found it. Look what I found. This sketchbook is dated 1819. Something's not right.

GERTIE. Do you need some painkillers?

KATHERINE. No. Something's bothering me in the research. It's in Schindler's biography. Here it is.

Schindler enters.

SCHINDLER. In May of 1822, the master rented a villa in Hetzendorf. The first composition Beethoven wrote there was the variations on Diabelli's waltz, which had taken his fancy in a curious way.

GERTIE. Yes?

KATHERINE. All of these sketches are dated from 1819.

GERTIE. So?

KATHERINE. So why does Schindler say Beethoven started working on them in 1822?

SCHINDLER. Diabelli had in the winter of 1822 invited Beethoven to compose a variation on his waltz.

KATHERINE. Diabelli proposed the variations in 1819. Schindler is wrong about that too.

GERTIE. Yes, there are many inaccuracies in Schindler's biography.

SCHINDLER. Soon after he declined Diabelli's invitation, Beethoven asked me to inquire how much Diabelli would pay for a set of variations. Diabelli was pleasantly surprised by the offer and immediately proposed eighty ducats.

Diabelli enters.

DIABELLI. Eighty ducats?!

SCHINDLER. In advance.

DIABELLI. In advance?!

SCHINDLER. Yes.

Diabelli exits.

KATHERINE. That's also wrong. This letter shows Beethoven himself negotiated with Diabelli for only forty ducats. And that's what he got paid.

GERTIE. I still don't know where you're headed with this.

KATHERINE. Beethoven began the piece in 1819. Why does Schindler only talk about 1822? I suspect Schindler wasn't there in 1819 when Beethoven began it.

GERTIE. OK. So what do you conclude from that?

KATHERINE. It was Schindler who started the legend that Beethoven hated Diabelli's waltz.

SCHINDLER. *(Trying to prove his point.)* The master did not care for the theme with its *Schusterfleck.*

KATHERINE. He is the only source that tells us that Beethoven found the theme commonplace. What if he wasn't even there? That means we truly have no idea what Beethoven thought of Diabelli's waltz.

He exits. Katherine crosses away from the table, frustrated.

GERTIE. Katherine, that is a true discovery.

KATHERINE. For two hundred years we have believed that Beethoven hated the waltz. Do you realize what a setback this is for me?

GERTIE. What are you talking about?

KATHERINE. What if, after all of this, he really wrote the variations for the money?

GERTIE. What?

KATHERINE. What if the reason was not artistic? What if he just wrote all these variations for the money? He needed the money?

GERTIE. Beethoven did like his money. But I don't think that's why he did it.

KATHERINE. What if he did it to outnumber Bach?

GERTIE. Bach?

KATHERINE. Yes! There are thirty-two movements in Bach's *Goldberg Variations.* Maybe Beethoven just wanted to one-up Bach. That's why he wrote thirty-three.

GERTIE. He did not say he was going to write thirty-three. At first he said he was only going to write six or seven. And then the number increased as his obsession grew.

KATHERINE. I've been here nine months now and I'm not any closer to figuring this out. Why he was obsessed with this mediocre waltz. I just don't get it.

GERTIE. Katherine, what's going on?

Pause.

KATHERINE. My tongue. My tongue has begun twitching.

GERTIE. When did it start?

KATHERINE. Two weeks ago. My tongue has begun to die.

Variation: "Cheeseburger"

Clara enters holding an "augmentative speech device"—a keyboard with a speaker built into it that will "speak" words or phrases that are typed on it. Mike follows.

CLARA. So how does it work?

MIKE. These buttons, you can program words and phrases.

CLARA. Show me.

Mike gets out a belt.

What are you doing?

MIKE. It helps if you are immobilized yourself when you learn how to use it.

It gives you a closer sense of what the patient—your mom, sorry—will have in terms of mobility.

CLARA. I see.

Mike ties Clara to the chair with his belt.

MIKE. Now touch here.

Clara presses a key on the keyboard.

MACHINE. Yes.

MIKE. Now here.

Clara does.

MACHINE. No.

MIKE. Here.

Clara does.

MACHINE. I want a cheeseburger.

Clara and Mike laugh.

CLARA. Pre-recorded words and pre-recorded phrases.

MIKE. Yes.

CLARA. Do you have any idea what this will do to her?

MIKE. I know. But they're not all pre-recorded. Try typing something.

Clara does.

MACHINE. Greetings Earthling.

Clara types.

You have bad hair.

Mike types.

Ouch.

MIKE. And I prerecorded this:

He presses a key.

MACHINE. And here's to you Mrs. Robinson.
Jesus loves you more than you will know.

Clara types.

Whoa, whoa, whoa.

They both laugh.

MIKE. And press this button.

MACHINE. I love you Clara.

Clara is silent.

MIKE. It's versatile. Huh. It even lets you say stupid things.

CLARA. *(Pointing to the belt around her.)* Do you really think this is the best way to tell me this?

MIKE. Clara, I don't have much in my life.

CLARA. Mike.

MIKE. Please hear me out.

I'm a nurse. I go to the hospital, I see bodies deteriorating all day long. I come home and go to bed.

It's not a fantastic life by any standards. But when I see you…

CLARA. I really don't want to talk about this.

MIKE. Let me finish. When I'm with you, you make the deteriorations of those bodies seem like something to look forward to.

Pause.

CLARA. Thank you?

MIKE. No! Not like that!

I am not good with words.

I see them and I wouldn't mind being them… I wouldn't mind having my body deteriorate like that, I think I could tolerate that, as long as I had some of my life with you.

Does that make sense?

Silence.

It's ridiculous, I know. I'm not good with words. I think if you think about deterioration, and what it does…

CLARA. Shut up.

MIKE. OK.

CLARA. That, that was the most beautiful thing anyone has ever said to me.

MIKE. Really?

CLARA. Everyone should have someone say something like that to them sometime.

MIKE. Really? *(In one breath.)* It sounded better in my head when I was thinking about it, with the bodies and the decomposition…

CLARA. Stop while you're ahead, though.

MIKE. Right.

Clara types.

MACHINE. And now will you please untie me.

Mike and Clara exit.

Variation: "Beauty"

Schindler enters, following Diabelli. Schindler holds an announcement of the publication of the other fifty variations. Diabelli carries boxes and letters.

SCHINDLER. Diabelli, you can't do this.

DIABELLI. Schindler, calm down.

SCHINDLER. If you publish the other composers' variations before the master's, it will be a terrible blow to him. He will be humiliated.

DIABELLI. He hasn't written a note on the variations in three years. I thought he had given up on the project entirely.

SCHINDLER. Well, he's working on it again.

DIABELLI. After three years?

SCHINDLER. Yes, after three years. For the last three months he's been working on it.

DIABELLI. Why didn't you tell me before?

SCHINDLER. Because I wasn't sure he was going to continue to work on it, but as soon as he finished the Ninth, he went back to it.

DIABELLI. Schindler. I'm sorry for him and for you. But I have an obligation to publish the other composers' variations. We can't wait any longer.

SCHINDLER. Diabelli, listen to me.

Last night, I was walking by his room and I heard melodies the likes of which I had never heard before. Beethoven has done exactly what he promised to do. The master has found a new language of composition. He is creating new forms of music and surpassing anything he's ever done before.

DIABELLI. And all that because of my waltz?

SCHINDLER. No, his work on the Mass seems to have opened new compositional landscapes to him.

Schindler removes a sketch from his coat pocket.

DIABELLI. What is that?

SCHINDLER. It's a sketch for Variation 31.

DIABELLI. *(Shocked.)* Thirty-one?

SCHINDLER. If he knew I took it, he'd kill me. But I needed to show it to you.

Schindler hands the sketch to Diabelli. Diabelli begins reading; the pianist plays Variation #31. Diabelli is obviously struck by its beauty.

DIABELLI. *(Over the music.)* Did you read this?

SCHINDLER. Yes.

DIABELLI. I can't believe this. I've never heard anything like it before.

These are my first four notes. And here he references my lower chords, and here the ascending notes…how magnificent!

SCHINDLER. And look at the back of the page.

The pianist plays Variation #22.

That's Variation number twenty-two.

DIABELLI. *(Over the music.)* A reference to *Don Giovanni*! Who knew I had Mozart in my waltz?

SCHINDLER. Do you recognize the melody?

DIABELLI. Yes.

SCHINDLER. And whose aria is that?

DIABELLI. It's Leporello's.

SCHINDLER. And what do we know about Leporello?

DIABELLI. He's Don Giovanni's servant. He's always…

Pause—he gets it.

He's always mocking his master.

SCHINDLER. Yes, but he serves him well.

Music stops.

DIABELLI. You and I are very much alike, Schindler.

SCHINDLER. In what way?

DIABELLI. We both love beauty, we both can recognize it. But neither of us can make it.

SCHINDLER. And that makes us both slaves to others.

DIABELLI. Indeed.

SCHINDLER. He needs more time.

DIABELLI. I have no more time.

Beethoven enters.

BEETHOVEN. Good afternoon!

Schindler hides the sketches behind his back.

DIABELLI. Luigi, what are you doing out in this weather?

BEETHOVEN. *(To Schindler.)* What are you doing here?

SCHINDLER. Nothing. Diabelli was inquiring about your health.

BEETHOVEN. What is the prognosis, doctor?

SCHINDLER. You should be in bed.

BEETHOVEN. What are you holding behind your back?

SCHINDLER. Nothing.

BEETHOVEN. Schindler! What are you holding behind your back?

SCHINDLER. Nothing, master!

BEETHOVEN. Go get the carriage ready. I want to talk to my friend alone.

Schindler leaves.

(Looking around.) Look at all this. You've done very well for yourself, Anton! It was only yesterday that you were a clerk at Steiner.

DIABELLI. Thank you. Yes.

BEETHOVEN. And now you're one of the most successful publishers in Vienna.

DIABELLI. *(Goes to write.)* It is only because…

BEETHOVEN. No, you don't have to write it down, I can read your lips.

DIABELLI. It is only because I publish composers like you. That's where my real wealth resides.

BEETHOVEN. And like Schubert, and like Liszt and like Weber…

DIABELLI. *(Smiling.)* Yes.

BEETHOVEN. You should get rid of all of them and publish only Beethoven.

DIABELLI. I agree.

BEETHOVEN. Schubert, you can keep Schubert. Discard the rest.

DIABELLI. You're very generous with Schubert.

BEETHOVEN. His songs are very pretty. But I heard he was arrested. *(Gleefully.)*

DIABELLI. Yes. For saying what we all think.

BEETHOVEN. I hear that Parliament is working on a new law that will lay down how high birds can fly.

DIABELLI. Be careful what you say, Luigi. The walls have ears.

BEETHOVEN. Freedom and progress! How can there be either freedom or progress with the police *(Yelling.)* listening to every word you say?

So, what did you think of my sketches?

DIABELLI. What sketches?

BEETHOVEN. The ones Schindler was trying to hide behind his back.

Diabelli smiles.

Those pages are my children. You think I wouldn't notice when one of them is kidnapped?

DIABELLI. Schindler is a loyal man.

BEETHOVEN. Your waltz is so…

DIABELLI. Yes?

BEETHOVEN. I'm not done yet, you know.

DIABELLI. Schindler told me.

BEETHOVEN. I need more time. *(Pleading.)* Anton. I need more time.

DIABELLI. I know.

BEETHOVEN. Promise me you won't publish the other composers' variations before mine.

DIABELLI. Of course, Luigi.
As long as it's within the next thirty days.

BEETHOVEN. *(Laughs.)* I can see how you got to be so rich.

Schindler enters. Beethoven gets up to leave.

SCHINDLER. Master, we should get you home.

DIABELLI. Luigi, I wanted to tell you I have a new cook.

BEETHOVEN. Yes?

DIABELLI. She makes the most delicious veal stew. I'll send you some today.

BEETHOVEN. Good, but tell her to make it thin—I can't digest anything thick anymore. I have gout of the chest, can you believe it?

DIABELLI. No.

BEETHOVEN. I didn't know such a thing existed and I have it.

DIABELLI. I thought that was a disease of the joints.

BEETHOVEN. Me too. Goodbye, Anton.

Beethoven walks to the door and then remembers something and returns.

I almost forgot. This is for you.

He takes a very large manuscript from the inside of his coat.

It's the Mass. It's finished.

He drops the manuscript of the Mass on the desk to the astonishment of Diabelli and Schindler. He turns and walks out. Schindler follows. Diabelli crosses to the table and sees what it is. He picks it up and begins to read. As he does we hear the music of the Mass. He bursts into laughter as he reads.

Variation: "Cafeteria Food"

Gertie, Clara, and Mike enter with trays. They are in line at the hospital cafeteria selecting their lunch.

CLARA. Did you get my mother her pills?

MIKE. Yes.

CLARA. OK. I finally found her arnica cream.

MIKE. Clara, you're doing an amazing job with your mother. Schnitzel?

GERTIE. Your mother is making great progress in her work. And it's in large part thanks to your help.

MIKE. It would be nice if she told *her* that.

GERTIE. *(To Clara.)* It's important not to want such things. If one expects them one is always disappointed, *ja?*

CLARA. *Ja?*

GERTIE. I've been thinking a lot about this. And I think it's time.

CLARA. Time for what?

GERTIE. Borscht, please. To get your mother a friend.

CLARA. A friend?

GERTIE. Yes, why? Do you think a woman with ALS has no sexual appetite?

CLARA. What?

GERTIE. Sauerkraut, please. Yes. Sexual appetite.

MIKE. Gertie, softer please. Everybody here speaks English.

GERTIE. There's nothing to be ashamed of. I think we should get your mother a masseur. A handsome masseur. She likes tall men she told me. We should get her a tall man. It is not very expensive.

CLARA. She told you she likes tall men? Noodles, please.

GERTIE. Yes. Tall is important to her. And black hair is preferable than blond.

CLARA. My mother's really opened up to you.

GERTIE. Sometimes it is easier to talk to someone who's not in the family.

CLARA. So she has she told you she wants you to hire a prostitute for her?

MIKE. Hey Clara, ix-nay on the rostitute-pay.

GERTIE. *Nein*, of course not. But that doesn't mean she wouldn't like it. She needs to feel healthy! When was the last time you had sex?

CLARA. Tuesday.

MIKE. Clara!

GERTIE. You see? My husband and I do it every Thursday and Tuesday. It's good for lower back pain.

CLARA. Where would we get someone like that?

GERTIE. On the Internet. There are pages and pages of prostitutes. We can look when we get back to the apartment.

CLARA. I think that's a great idea.

GERTIE. Good.

MIKE. I don't want to know about this.

GERTIE. I understand. He's seen your mother naked. So he doesn't want to think about that.

MIKE. No! It's not that.

GERTIE. It's OK. Clara and I will choose the man. You don't have to worry.

MIKE. I'm not worried.

GERTIE. I think he should be a Turkish man. They are very good with women.

CLARA. *(Amused.)* Really?

GERTIE. *Ja, sehr gut.* They take their time.

MIKE. OK. I have enough food.

Mike exits.

GERTIE. Or he could be Brazilian. I will google.

Variation: "Fugue"

Beethoven is in his room. He's composing. He is in his own world.

BEETHOVEN. I know.
A fugue. It must be a fugue.
I must conquer the fugue.
For three independent voices in staggered entrances.

The pianist plays the fugue, Variation #32 in C Major.

No not in C major.

No, definitely not in C major. It must be a foreign key. One never used before in the whole set. A variation that exists far from the theme.

The music begins slowly, tentatively in E-flat major.

Yes, in E-flat major.

...and let it expand.
...Now let it sink to
the low register.
...Now quicker in different keys:
C minor,
piu mosso
...E-flat major,
...F minor,
...C minor,
...Crescendo!
cresc.
...Forte!

59
...In octaves!
ff
65
sf
...Now invert them.
71
...And invert them again.
77
...And double it.
...And double it again.
83
...Shhhh, whisper.
sf
sf
p
...whisper.
sf
sf

89
95
...Sforzando
...Now let it expand.
...Let it soar.
ff
sf
101
...In the style of the great Handel.
107
...I still have so much to learn from Handel.
112

And now it starts again, twice as fast.
Three subjects simultaneously.
l. hand
sf

sempre p

Bring it down to the low A flat...

...And now bring the subject up to the high F.
sempre p

136
...crescendo...
cresc.
140
...Fortissimo.
ff
144
And now the closing.
sempre ff
148
...the world is condensing, refining itself.
152

Fugue finishes. Lights change and the pianist plays Variation #25.

Variation: "Morphine"

Gertie, Katherine, and Clara sit at a beautiful outdoor café. As the lights come up, they are laughing. Katherine is now in an electric wheelchair. Clara feeds her soup.

KATHERINE. Here's a story. Three pianists meet on a train.

GERTIE. Is this going to be a joke?

KATHERINE. No, it's not a joke.

GERTIE. Because I do not like jokes.

KATHERINE. It's not a joke.

GERTIE. Good. Because I do not like jokes.

KATHERINE. Gertie!

Pause.

Three pianists meet on a train. After some conversation they realize that they all had recently played Beethoven's Third Concerto. And one of the pianists says, "It's strange; whenever I play that concerto, I keep seeing the image of a woman in a red dress." And to his surprise, the other two pianists said that every time they play the concerto, they too see the image of a woman in a red dress.

CLARA. That's a great story.

KATHERINE. I know. Isn't that amazing?

GERTIE. *Ja*, it is.

Pause.

Clara, I just want to tell you that I'll be there for you and your mother. For what comes next.

KATHERINE. Gertie, please not now.

GERTIE. Sorry Katherine, but I want her to know I'll be here for her.

CLARA. Thank you, Gertie.

GERTIE. And I want to make sure you're comfortable with Katherine's plans.

CLARA. I don't have much choice with her plans.

GERTIE. So you're OK with your mother's wishes for the end.

KATHERINE. Gertie. Not now.

CLARA. What?

GERTIE. You didn't tell her?

KATHERINE. It's not time yet.

GERTIE. Oh my! I'm so sorry, Clara.

CLARA. No please, go ahead, tell me.

Gertie pauses; looks at Katherine.

KATHERINE. Go ahead. Finish what you started.

GERTIE. Well, your mother has given me very strict instructions about the end. I was sure you knew. I'm so sorry.

CLARA. Gertie, just tell me.

GERTIE. She wants to be kept alive until she can't communicate anymore. Then after that she wants to be given morphine and left to die.

CLARA. *(Deeply hurt and angry.)* I can't believe this.

GERTIE. Clara, this is a very personal decision. And your mother has given it a great deal of thought.

KATHERINE. I want to live. But only while I can still communicate. If I cannot make myself understood, I want to be given morphine and left to die. I want that to be clear.

CLARA. And you couldn't tell me this? You had to tell Gertie?

KATHERINE. I need someone more objective who can take care of these things.

CLARA. I see.

Pause.

And who will be administering the morphine?

KATHERINE. Gertie has agreed to do it.

CLARA. And she'll decide when that should occur.

KATHERINE. Yes.

CLARA. You've decided everything, Mom. Congratulations. Should I come see you at the hospital?

KATHERINE. Don't be childish, Clara. I am doing you a favor so that you won't have to make these decisions.

CLARA. What happens if after you can't communicate you change your mind and you want to go on living?

KATHERINE. That won't happen.

CLARA. How will Gertie get the morphine?

KATHERINE. We asked Mike to get it for us.

CLARA. Mike?

KATHERINE. Yes. He did. She has it already.

CLARA. He didn't tell me anything.

KATHERINE. He couldn't. I'm his patient.

CLARA. *(Very wounded by this.)* Very well, then. You've figured all of it out now. Good for you, Mom.

KATHERINE. Clara, don't make a scene.

Pause.

CLARA. A scene?!

KATHERINE. It's my decision, and I don't want to talk about this any more.

Pause. Clara gets up.

CLARA. Who has cooked your dinner every night? Who has cleaned your clothes—cleaned *you?* Who has made it possible for you to spend all these months here to work on your precious monograph?
I'm good enough for all that, but not the big decisions?
I finally see how you see me, Mom. And it's horrible.

She exits.

KATHERINE. *(To Gertie.)* Thank you very much.

GERTIE. I can't believe you hadn't told her.

KATHERINE. I didn't want to burden her with it.

GERTIE. You are too smart a woman to lie to yourself.

KATHERINE. Clara brings the illness with her.

GERTIE. What?

KATHERINE. You see a musicologist. She sees an invalid.

GERTIE. She sees her mother.
In fact, it is you who cannot see your daughter.

KATHERINE. Stop playing psychologist.

GERTIE. I'm your friend.

KATHERINE. You are a kind acquaintance.

Pause.

And you shouldn't have said anything.

GERTIE. Very well, then. I am a kind acquaintance then. And you think of your daughter as a second-rate waltz. The waltz is mediocre. Your daughter is mediocre. Everything you don't understand is mediocre. Goodbye.

KATHERINE. Gertie, where are you going?
You can't leave me alone.

GERTIE. You're not alone. You can call your daughter.
Goodbye.

Gertie exits.

KATHERINE. Gertie! Gertie!

Katherine tries to back up from the table, but her wheelchair is caught on a leg. She turns to call a waitress.

Fraulein! Fraulein! Fraulein!

No one comes. Katherine becomes furious and aware of her prison. She cries bitterly. She begins coughing and then choking. We hear an ambulance in the background.

Variation: "Intimacy"

Mike has fallen asleep on the bed he shares with Clara in the Bonn apartment with a book on his chest. Clara enters and begins to undress quietly. Mike wakes up.

MIKE. How is she?

CLARA. She's OK. It was just a scare. She started choking and couldn't get rid of the phlegm and she panicked and the waiters called an ambulance. The doctor cleared her throat and said she'll be fine.

MIKE. Good.

CLARA. They wanted to keep her overnight at the hospital, but she refused. So I brought her home. She's asleep now. She's furious at Gertie.

Pause.

Her hands were really cramping. They look so small. I massaged them and she felt a little better.

MIKE. Good.

CLARA. The irony is that we were never a very physical family. And now, all we do is touch.

MIKE. Yes, that's one of the benefits of ALS. It forces intimacy.

CLARA. What are the other benefits?

Clara sits on a chair next to the bed. She is in her underwear and a tank top. Mike crosses to her and tries to touch her. Clara's back goes up. She pulls away and says:

I haven't forgiven you yet.

MIKE. OK.

He withdraws. Pause.

I couldn't tell you. I'm her nurse.

CLARA. I thought you were here for me.

MIKE. I have to respect her wishes.

CLARA. How long have you known.

MIKE. Two weeks.

CLARA. Two weeks? Don't think she respects you just because you got her the morphine. She doesn't.

MIKE. I don't care what she thinks. You're the one who cares so much about what she thinks.

CLARA. Thank you.

MIKE. Is this about me getting her the morphine? Or is it about the fact that she's dying.

Small pause.

Because she's dying.

CLARA. I know that. I'm so stupid.

I thought if I came here, somehow, she and I would be able to figure things out.

MIKE. Well what if that doesn't happen?

CLARA. What?

MIKE. I see people go through this all the time. Everybody wants some kind of closure before the end. But it doesn't work that way. It never happens the way people want it to happen.

CLARA. Then what am I doing here?

MIKE. You're spending time with your mother. You're taking care of her, feeding her, bathing her. And that might be what you get. I'm sorry you found out like that. But those moments with your mom, that might be what you get.

CLARA. This fucking disease.

MIKE. This fucking disease.

CLARA. Can we please have sex?

MIKE. Why?

CLARA. Why?

MIKE. No. Not why? I think it's a great idea. Yep. Fantastic idea. Let's do it.

CLARA. *(Laughs.)* I just… I just want to feel healthy. Is that a horrible thing to say?

MIKE. No, it's not. I will make you feel super healthy. You'll see how healthy we can be.

They laugh. He leans in and kisses her. They begin to undress as… The pianist plays Variation #24 …

Katherine enters in her wheelchair on the other side of the stage. The music continues to play as she speaks and the lovers continue exploring their bodies.

KATHERINE. This is Variation #24. It begins the final movement of the variations.

Beethoven's beginning to bring the entire project to a close. There's such tenderness to his departure.

There's no arrogance. No regrets. Instead, a gentle procession into uncharted territories.

He still has some thoughts. There are nine variations yet to come. But the bulk of the work is done.

Long pause.

How does one begin to let go?

End playing music.

Variation: "A Peace Offering"

It's late at night, days later. Gertie and Katherine are studying books and sketches in Katherine's kitchen.

GERTIE. OK. That's it. I can't look at notes anymore. I'm going home.

KATHERINE. Yes. Go. You've been here too long. And thank you for everything.

GERTIE. *Bitte schön.*

You should go to sleep. You'll be more productive tomorrow.

CLARA. Oh sorry, I didn't know you were still working.

GERTIE. No, no problem.

I'm leaving. I'm done for the night.

Gertie starts packing up her things.

CLARA. Good night, Gertie.

GERTIE. Good night.

CLARA. Wait. *(Very shocked.)* Is that a sketchbook?

GERTIE. *(Caught.) Ja.*

CLARA. You took it from the library?

GERTIE. *Ja.* And now I am taking it back.

CLARA. Gertie! You could go to jail for that. You are breaking the law?

GERTIE. I am living for danger.

Clara laughs.

And besides, it was a peace offering. After your mother sent me flowers and a kilo of pigs' knuckles.

KATHERINE. Can I keep the peace offering for a few more days?

GERTIE. *(Handing her back the book.)* If Mohammed doesn't go to the mountain, the mountain comes to Mohammed.

OK. I'll see you all tomorrow.

Clara rifles through the cupboard for tea and sugar. She begins to sing the waltz. Katherine and Gertie look at each other in surprise.

KATHERINE. Clara, what are you doing?

CLARA. Making some tea, do you want some?

KATHERINE. No. Keep singing.

CLARA. Are you being sarcastic?

KATHERINE. No, please…

Katherine looks at her. Clara sings the waltz.

Do you know what you're singing?

CLARA. Yes. It's Diabelli's waltz, isn't it?

KATHERINE. Yes. But why are you singing it?

CLARA. I like it.
Why is that wrong?

KATHERINE. It's not wrong.
What do you like about it?

CLARA. Gertie, sing the waltz.

Gertie starts singing the waltz.

It has a pretty melody. It has a nice rhythm.

The theme begins to play slowly.

See, it's pretty.

GERTIE. Yes. She has a point.

CLARA. You can feel the rhythm. Gertie, mark the rhythm.

Gertie begins to tap the table; she gets into the rhythm of it.

GERTIE. It's not a concert hall waltz, it's a beer hall waltz.

Gertie gets more and more into the music, pounding the table and stomping her feet. Clara and Katherine watch with amusement. Gertie stops and looks at Clara. The music stops.

Clara. Good point. That's a fine musicological observation.

CLARA. I don't know about that. I find the waltz pretty. That's all.

Katherine is looking at Clara as if for the first time.

What?

KATHERINE. Nothing…

Suddenly, Katherine starts choking.

CLARA. Mom? Mom?

Blackout; the pianist plays Variation #27.

Variation: "Not a Human Being"

Beethoven is in his study. He hasn't been out in days. He looks like a decrepit old man. He is agitated and composing in his head. He opens his pants and starts urinating on the floor. Schindler enters and sees Beethoven.

SCHINDLER. Master, no! Master!

The music stops. Schindler rushes to get cloths to wipe up, then ushers Beethoven back to his table and sits him down.

Master, the doctor said YOU SHOULD REST.

Beethoven reads his lips.

BEETHOVEN. No.

SCHINDLER. You're sick. We'll put you to bed.

BEETHOVEN. No!

SCHINDLER. You are only human.

BEETHOVEN. I must NOT be a human being.
I must not be for myself alone.

SCHINDLER. Master, you must not tempt fate.

BEETHOVEN. *(Yelling.)* I shall take fate by the throat and bend it to my will.

SCHINDLER. I am sending for the doctor.

BEETHOVEN. *(For the first time truly terrified.)* No, no, no more doctors, please! No more doctors!

SCHINDLER. You leave me no choice.

BEETHOVEN. *(Pointing to the sketches.)* Don't you see?
This music will free people from all the misery and all the indignities that shackle them.

SCHINDLER. Master.

BEETHOVEN. I am an instrument of G_d! I am Bacchus who creates the most glorious wine for mankind and makes them spiritually drunken! I will heal the wounds of the world.

SCHINDLER. Master, please! You're losing your mind!

BEETHOVEN. You putrid appendix! You were a second violinist in a fifth-rate orchestra! How can you, being so vulgar, appreciate anything that's not vulgar? Having you around makes it impossible to compose. Leave my sight at once.

Beethoven has a severe pain that almost makes him collapse.

SCHINDLER. Master, please sit, sit. Wait here.
I'll get a warm compress.

On the other side of the stage, Katherine is revealed on a gurney about to enter an MRI machine. A live projection of her face, filmed from above, appears behind her. The voice of the nurse is heard over a speaker.

NURSE. OK, Dr. Brandt, can you hear me?

KATHERINE. Yes.

NURSE. Good.

I will be out here looking at the monitor and making sure everything is OK. And I will talk to you through the speakers.

KATHERINE. That's fine.

NURSE. Once the table slides into the machine and we begin the tests, the noise will be quite loud. But I will be able to hear you if you need to speak.

On the other side of the stage, Mike and Clara are sitting in a waiting room. Gertie enters and gives Clara a kiss on the cheek.

GERTIE. How are you doing?

CLARA. I'm OK.

GERTIE. Hello, Mike.

MIKE. Hi.

GERTIE. How is Katherine doing?

MIKE. The doctors are with her now.

GERTIE. What time is it? *(Looking at her watch.)* Clara, do you want to go get some sleep after this? I can stay here.

CLARA. No, thank you.

GERTIE. You've been up for more than twenty-four hours.

CLARA. I'm OK. I told her I would be here when she woke up.

GERTIE. OK. But I'll take tomorrow night.

NURSE. So, here we go into the machine. Try to keep as still as you can.

There is the sound of Katherine being moved into the machine. The pianist begins to play D slow octave tremolo, which underscores the scene.

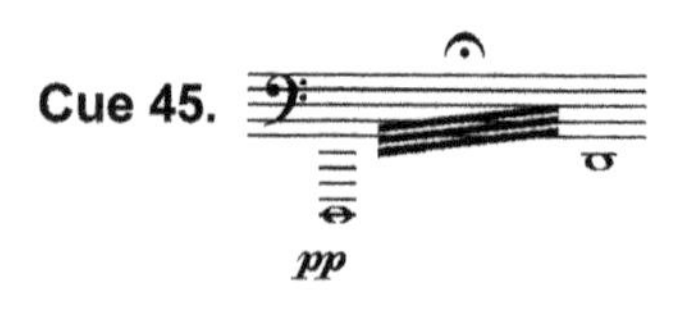

CLARA. She's been choking so much lately.

GERTIE. Yes.

CLARA. And she gets so scared that she'll choke to death on her own saliva. I keep telling her it won't happen. But…

MIKE. It's not going to happen.

CLARA. Gertie, how did your aunt die?

GERTIE. That was how she died.

The magnitude of what awaits them hits Clara. She begins to cry.

CLARA. Really?

GERTIE. Yes.

She stands and moves away from Mike and Gertie. Schindler comes back into Beethoven's room.

SCHINDLER. Master. Here, take this. Rest. I'll go get you a blanket.

BEETHOVEN. No. Please. Stay. Don't leave me.

NURSE. Very well, please hold your breath.

The sound of the MRI machine is heard.

BEETHOVEN. Lord, have mercy.

Sound of MRI machine is heard.

CLARA. Lord, have mercy.

Sound of MRI machine is heard.

KATHERINE. *Kyrie eleison.*

Sound of MRI machine is heard.

SCHINDLER. *(Sings.) Kyrie…*

Piano tremolo stops.

CLARA. *(Sings.) Kyrie…*

Diabelli enters reading a copy of the Mass.

DIABELLI. *(Sings.)* Kyrie…

KATHERINE. *(Sings.) Kyrie eleison…*

Katherine, Clara, Schindler, and Diabelli sing the beginning of the "Kyrie" portion of Beethoven's Mass in four-part harmony. It is a meditative and prayerful moment in which they have left the reality of their surroundings and search for comfort in the beauty of the music. They are all in need of a merciful G_d. As the music ends, wind is heard, Clara falls asleep on Mike's shoulder. Schindler and Diabelli exit. Beethoven crosses to Katherine's bedside.

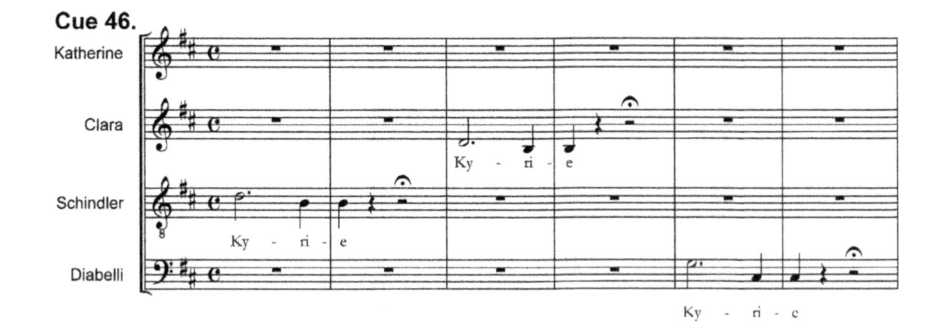

Assai moderato
K.
C.
S.
D.
Ky - - - ri - e e - lei - - - son, e - lei - - -
e - lei - - -
e - lei - - -
cresc.
son. Ky - - - ri - e, Ky - - - ri -
son, Ky - - ri-e e - lei - - -
e - lei - - - son, Ky - - - ri - e e - lei - - -
son, e - lei - - - - son. Ky - - - - ri-e e - lei - - -

13
K.
e e - lei - - - son. Ky - - ri - e e - lei - - -
C.
son, e - lei - - - son. e - lei - - -
S.
son, e - lei - - - son. e - lei - - -
D.
son, e - lei - - - son. e -
p
sf
19
K.
- - son, Ky - ri - e e - lei - son, e - lei - son.
C.
- - son. Ky - ri - e e - lei - son, e - lei - son.
S.
- - son. Ky - ri - e e - lei - son, e - lei - son.
D.
lei - son. Ky - ri - e e - lei - son, e - lei - son.
cresc.

Variation: "Limbo"

KATHERINE. *(Music ends. Noticing Beethoven.)* Oh no! I was so hoping I wouldn't hallucinate. It doesn't look good in a scholar.

BEETHOVEN. It could have been worse.

KATHERINE. How?

BEETHOVEN. It could have been Tchaikovsky.

KATHERINE. I'm not a Tchaikovsky scholar.

BEETHOVEN. No. You're a Beethoven scholar.

KATHERINE. Tchaikovsky comes after you. How do you know about him?

BEETHOVEN. We're in limbo together.

KATHERINE. Why are you in limbo?

BEETHOVEN. We all fled heaven. The angelic music made me wish I was still deaf.

Katherine smiles.

All of us are in limbo. Mozart, Bach, Schubert. They're very upset with us in heaven.

Pause.

I can see you're not getting better.

KATHERINE. Thank you.

BEETHOVEN. I can see you're not getting better.

KATHERINE. I know that. So what?

BEETHOVEN. I started going deaf in 1797.

KATHERINE. I know.

BEETHOVEN. I was completely deaf by 1822.

KATHERINE. I know.

BEETHOVEN. It took me twenty-five years to go deaf.

KATHERINE. I know.

BEETHOVEN. Here's something you don't know: One day my hearing would be bad, and I would be terrified of going completely deaf. The next day it would improve. And my hope would return. And then it would get worse again. This back-and-forth between hope and despair was unbearable. And then, after twenty-five years of this, I became completely deaf. All hope was gone. And I was so…relieved! I would never hope again. Hoping is the great curse. And lo and behold, I was able to create music that would have never been possible had I been in the world of the hearing. The thing I'd feared most had happened and yet it allowed me to be with my music in the most intimate of ways.

KATHERINE. *(Triumphant.)* I suspected that. I wrote a paper and I made that point.

BEETHOVEN. You were right.

KATHERINE. *(Delighted.)* I knew it.

BEETHOVEN. You were right.

KATHERINE. I knew it.

BEETHOVEN. Dr. Brandt, it's time. It's time to stop struggling.

Katherine is overcome by tears. She knows Beethoven is right.

KATHERINE. I am so jealous.

BEETHOVEN. Of whom?

KATHERINE. Of everyone who will continue.

BEETHOVEN. I was so jealous of everyone who could hear.

KATHERINE. All the time.

BEETHOVEN. All the time.

Gertie coughs. Beethoven notices Clara, Mike, and Gertie in the waiting room.

Who is that?

KATHERINE. That's my friend, Gertie. She's devoted her life to taking care of your sketches.

BEETHOVEN. No, no. The other one. The younger one.

KATHERINE. That's my daughter, Clara.

BEETHOVEN. She's the one who wanders.

KATHERINE. Yes.

BEETHOVEN. What a brave girl.

KATHERINE. *(Crying.)* Yes. She's a handful.

BEETHOVEN. What is the problem?

KATHERINE. I've had so much in my life. I want her to be happy in hers.

BEETHOVEN. Why do you think she's not?

Lights change, second half of Diabelli's theme plays triumphantly along with the sound of applause. Diabelli appears in his most festive—if somewhat pompous—clothing, holding a beautifully bound book in his hand. Applause is heard.

DIABELLI. *(Speaking to a large public.)* Today we present to the world this beautiful book: a set of 33 variations, penned by our own Viennese composer Ludwig van Beethoven!

Applause.

With this work, we offer the world a true masterpiece as only our finest composer can produce.

KATHERINE. Look at that.

He seems very happy with your composition. Are you?

BEETHOVEN. I could have used another couple of weeks.

Pause.

Why is it that they always look like that and I always look like this?

DIABELLI. These variations are made still more intriguing by the fact that they were based on a waltz of my own making

Pause. He becomes overwhelmed.

that no one else believed held such promise.

Never did I think that my humble waltz would inspire such a magnificent work. This is, without a doubt, the greatest set of variations ever written.

Applause, lights change.

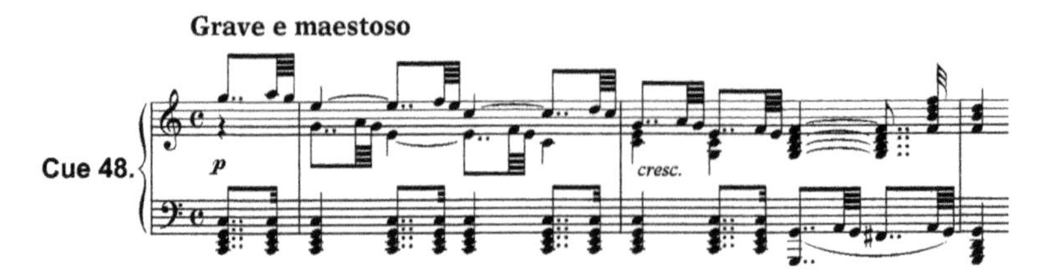

Variation: "Breakfast"

As the music ends, Katherine is in a hospital bed. Clara is sitting on the couch reading a novel. Mike is in a chair asleep. There are pages from Katherine's monograph strewn about. Gertie stands next to Katherine and holds a page for her to read. Katherine's speech has become labored as the illness is paralyzing her tongue.

KATHERINE. It's good.

GERTIE. *(Putting that page in a stack.)* Good. So that's chapter nine.
And twelve you saw already.

KATHERINE. Yes.

GERTIE. And eight I checked and it's fine.

KATHERINE. And the introduction?

CLARA. I checked it. They proposed changes to the second-to-last paragraph.

KATHERINE. Uh-uh.

CLARA. I know, I told them to leave it as is.

KATHERINE. Good.

GERTIE. OK, I'll take these to the post office.
And then we only have two more chapters to go.

KATHERINE. Thank you, Gertie.

GERTIE. *Bitte schön. (To Clara, blowing her a kiss.)* Bye.

She exits. Uncomfortable silence. Mike snores.

KATHERINE. He can sleep through anything, that one can.

CLARA. Yes. I wish I could sleep through his snoring.

Pause.

KATHERINE. You've been here all day. Did you eat?

CLARA. Yes. Thank you. Mike and I had a big breakfast.

KATHERINE. What did you have? Details.

CLARA. *Brötchen mit* strawberry preserves.

KATHERINE. Yum.

Pause. Mike snores.

I think he loves you.

CLARA. Yes.

KATHERINE. How do you feel?

CLARA. The same.

KATHERINE. Good.

Pause.

CLARA. He has to get back to New York next week.

KATHERINE. What about you?

CLARA. I'm staying.

KATHERINE. I don't want to interrupt your life.

CLARA. Mom, I was planning on staying, but if you want me to go, I understand, I'll go.

Pause.

KATHERINE. No.

Pause.

Don't go.

CLARA. Okay.

Pause.

Clara understands. Mike snores.

KATHERINE. My G_d! That is so annoying!!!

Pause.

Clara, my nose is itching.

Clara goes to Katherine and scratches her nose.

CLARA. Here?

Katherine mumbles something.

Here?

She finds the spot.

KATHERINE. Mmmmm. Harder. Mmmmm. More.

CLARA. Do you want to scratch it yourself?

KATHERINE. Yes.

Clara holds up Katherine's hand and helps Katherine scratch her own nose. Katherine loves it. She's so relieved. Finally Clara stops. Katherine and Clara see each other. Clara begins to cry. Katherine too. Intimacy...

Variation: "Variation #33"

ANNOUNCER. And now ladies and gentlemen, without further ado, it is my great, great pleasure to introduce to you the keynote speaker of this conference, our esteemed colleague Dr. Katherine Brandt.

Katherine gets up from her bed. She's perfectly healthy.

KATHERINE. As scholars, we begin our search with an hypothesis and then take the necessary steps to prove or disprove it.

My hypothesis was that Beethoven wanted to use Diabelli's waltz to show Vienna what a great masterwork he could create out of a grain of sand.

My hypothesis was not insubstantial or far-fetched. It was simply incorrect.

You see, I didn't see in that waltz what Beethoven saw in it.

I saw it as an inconsequential trifle, the way it has been viewed for the past two hundred years.

But Beethoven saw it for what it was: a beer-hall waltz!

People danced to it.

I propose that Beethoven was not trying to make something out of nothing; instead, he was showing us what lies in every moment of the waltz.

He takes the first four notes in the opening of the waltz and makes six variations with them.

The repeated chord in the treble gives birth to two more variations.

The ascending notes generate five more.

So that a fifty-second waltz yields a fifty-minute composition.

Variation form allows Beethoven to do the miraculous and slow down time, to pierce the waltz and enter the minutiae that life, in its haste, robs us of.

There's the moment when your hand first graces the hand of your dance partner.

There's the moment when your eyes meet, a moment of trepidation as the music begins.

He smells good,
she's missed a step,
does she like me,
does he wish I were a better dancer,
and so on.

So that for Beethoven, variation form is not only a musical structure, it is a way to reclaim all that is fleeting. Allowing us to see it with new eyes.

Pause.

My daughter was in my hospital room today. She looked at her boyfriend, and for one second I saw such strength in her eyes. And I saw the lives they'll share, and I saw the mistakes they'll make, and I saw the way they'll raise their children. It was something.

Pause.

And so we arrive at the final variation.

Beethoven chooses to end the set of variations with a minuet. A graceful dance.

And I find such beautiful symmetry in his design.

We start with a beer-hall waltz and end with a delicate, spiritual dance.

Variations on a dance should end with a dance.

What an elegant idea—and so eloquently articulated by the master.

Clara appears dressed in very formal attire and holding the pages of the lecture she's been delivering.

This from a man who could not dance.

Katherine stops speaking as Clara continues. Then she slowly exits.

CLARA. "This from a man who could not dance.

I have asked my daughter to deliver this paper to you. And I want to thank her for agreeing to do it. She was instrumental in helping me write it.

This is indeed my final lecture. I want to thank you for being my colleagues. I am honored to have had you as my peers."

Smiling, she puts the paper down.

That's it. That's the end of her paper.

As many of you may know, my mother passed away three weeks ago, in the middle of the night.

Per her request, she was buried in Bonn. We all appreciated the messages you sent. Thank you.

She wanted me to end her lecture by reading a quote of Beethoven's himself.

She looks at the last page of the lecture.

Here it is:

Beethoven enters and says:

BEETHOVEN. "Let us begin with the primary cause of things.
Let us begin with how something came about.
Why it came about in that particular way
and became what it is."

Applause in the lecture hall. Gertie enters with the sketchbook that contains the variations. She looks at it. The last variation begins to play.

pp
sempre pp
p
cresc.
f

As the music plays, a projection reads "Variation #33." She places the sketchbook in its box and then takes the box to the shelf where it belongs. She places it there and takes off her gloves. The shelf recedes into the dozen other shelves. We become aware of the magnitude of Beethoven's work. As the shelf recedes, Mike, Diabelli, and Schindler enter. They join Clara and Beethoven, who have stayed onstage from the end of the lecture. It's a funeral of sorts. As the shelf arrives at its final position, the whole company begins a slow cross upstage. And then, unexpectedly, facing upstage, they all begin to do the steps of the minuet. It is very ritualistic at first: Each person dancing the steps on his/her own. As the music grows in emotion, they all make a circle, the present and the past finally together. They dance with each other and then exchange partners. Katherine enters the group and joins this circle. As the music begins to end, all the characters approach the sides of the stage, leaving Katherine and Beethoven alone in the center. As the music ends, everyone but those two leave the stage. Beethoven and Katherine look at each other and slowly cross towards the audience as if they were about to begin their discussions in earnest. As this cross commences, the lights begin to fade to black. Then, the last chord plays with the blackout.

End of Play

Wanna know how Tectonic Theater Project creates its plays?
Workshops and Resources to Support Your Production

Dedicated to challenging traditional theatrical form, Tectonic sends its company members all over the country to lead training labs in Moment Work, Tectonic's devised theater technique. In Moment Work, collaborators explore theatrical possibilities by investigating the narrative potential of lights, props, sound, costume, movement, and architecture. Once rich images are constructed, collaborators find or write the dialogue that the theatrical explorations inspire.

Tectonic Theater Project also offers the following services:

—Lectures and discussions delivered by Moisés Kaufman and Tectonic Company members
—Live or virtual Q & A sessions with Tectonic Company members
—Other events and programs to benefit your school, group, or production!

You can also engage with Tectonic through Facebook, Twitter, YouTube, Vimeo, and Flickr.

Interested in learning more? Contact us at:
education@tectonictheaterproject.org, or
212-579-6111

PROPERTY LIST

Purse
Tray of food
Half-packed suitcase, clothes
Laptops
Tickets
Suitcases
Books
Sketchbooks, books, catalogues
Gloves
Cell phones
Bowl of soup
Sketchbook, pen
Sketches
Note
Newspaper clipping
Gurney
Cane, walker
Bowl and washcloth
Pocketwatch
Notebook, pen
Keyboard with speaker
Belt, chair
Announcement
Boxes, letters
Manuscript
Cafeteria trays
Bowl of soup, spoon
Cloths
Beautifully bound book
Papers

SOUND EFFECTS

Offstage whispering
Loud metal bang
Loudspeaker announcements
Airplane taking off
Flight attendant announcements
Train passing
Nightclub music
Ringing distortion
Sounds of X-ray machine
Thunder and rain
Amplified breathing
Machine speaking
Beethoven's Mass
Ambulance
MRI machine
Applause

NOTES

(Use this space to make notes for your production)